D1013283

THE SELF-MADE
BILLIONAIRE
EFFECT

THE SELF-MADE
BILLIONAIRE
EFFECT

HOW EXTREME PRODUCERS
CREATE MASSIVE VALUE

JOHN SVIOKLA
MITCH COHEN

PORTFOLIO / PENGUIN

PORTFOLIO / PENGUIN
Published by the Penguin Group
Penguin Group (USA) LLC
375 Hudson Street
New York, New York 10014

USA | Canada | UK | Ireland | Australia | New Zealand | India | South Africa | China
penguin.com
A Penguin Random House Company

First published by Portfolio / Penguin, a member of Penguin Group (USA) LLC, 2014

Copyright © 2014 by PricewaterhouseCoopers. LLP

hardcover ISBN: 978-1-59184-763-2
export ISBN: 978-1-59184-782-3

Printed in the United States of America
1 3 5 7 9 10 8 6 4 2

Set in Life LT Std and Knockout
Designed by Jaime Putorti

John Sviokla:

To my children, John, Michael, Patrick, Kathleen, Kevin, and daughter-in-law, Lizzie, whose passion for engaging ideas— even those in this book—always inspires me. And most of all to my sweetie, Eileen, who is the wisest, most patient and loving soul I'll ever know.

Mitch Cohen:

For my wife, Carri, for standing beside me my entire career, encouraging me when I needed it, and bringing me down to earth when I needed that! And to my children, Alex and Lauren, for always making me proud and, most important, for always making me smile. I love you all.

CONTENTS

THE SELF-MADE
BILLIONAIRE
EFFECT

INTRODUCTION

Whenever you find yourself on the side of the majority,
it is time to pause and reflect.
—MARK TWAIN

Imagine what Atari might have achieved in the early 1980s if Steve Jobs had worked *inside* to develop the first mass-market personal computer? What might Steve Case have done for PepsiCo if he had decided to stay rather than join the gaming start-up that would eventually become AOL? Would Redken have been the first hair care brand to explode the market for salon-quality hair products if John Paul Mitchell Systems cofounder John Paul DeJoria had not been fired for his unconventional sales leadership style? Would Miles Laboratories have succeeded if it had pursued the idea posed by Michael Jaharis, then a young lawyer in its ranks, to proactively brand and market acetaminophen years before Tylenol became a household name? What if Salomon Brothers had kept Michael Bloomberg, or Bear Stearns had exploited the inventive ideas of Stephen Ross?

Jobs, Case, DeJoria, Jaharis, Bloomberg, and Ross, as well as Broadcast.com founder Mark Cuban, Celtel founder Mo Ibrahim, oil-and-gas magnate T. Boone Pickens, and scores of other extreme entrepreneurs all worked for established corporations before they struck out on their own. Some fled corporate constraints. Others were pushed out. Each one became a self-made billionaire. They all built businesses—in some cases multiple businesses—that are among the most iconic brands today. The influence of these and the roughly eight hundred other living self-made billionaires is so widespread that few people anywhere in the world can go a day without using, seeing, or in some way encountering the products and services they have created.

But what might their former employers have become if these exceptional value creators had decided to pursue and produce their ideas inside the organizations? Put a different way, why aren't existing corporations able to create massive value the way these self-made billionaires have? In so many cases, large corporations had the literal talent necessary do so—the self-made billionaires worked for them.

That latter question is top of mind for today's business leaders—smart, experienced, successful managers who are seeing their organizations pushed to the limits by rapid change. In today's environment all the base assumptions of how to build and sustain value are constantly in flux: What makes for efficient scale? Who are our competitors? Who are our customers? What do they want? Who owns what? Where is the risk? In a recent CEO survey conducted by PwC, more than half of the respondents predicted they would need to change their strategy either incrementally or wholesale in the coming years. Nearly 70 percent of those same respondents said they were concerned about talent issues, and 25 percent did not pursue a clear opportunity in the past year because they *believed* they didn't have the talent to take advantage of it.[1] The fact that so many self-made billionaires held managerial positions in midsize to large firms before striking out on their own suggests that the survey respondents just might be wrong about this issue. They have the talent but haven't taken the time to identify or nurture it.

Taken together, these responses make clear that business leaders are uncertain about how to tackle the particular challenge of continually creating value in today's environment. Throughout their careers these leaders have taken care to cultivate and promote managers with sound judgment—that celebrated ability to see the world as it is and to make smart, strategic decisions based on reality. Judgment works best when the rules of the game are well established, when the variables are known. But what do you do in a changing world where the variables keep shifting?

To answer that question we decided to look more closely at the leaders and the businesses that have thrived in our era of constant change. Despite the challenges of the day, despite the apparent mismatch between available skills and huge opportunities, there is a group of people creating value at an explosive pace and scale—*self-made* billionaires. We defined self-made billionaires as those individuals who create wealth of more than $1 billion through entrepreneurial activity; even those who inherited some financial resources or an existing business can qualify as self-made if they expand the value of that resource on the order of 100X or more.

In 2012, there were more than eight hundred self-made billionaires worldwide; they made up more than two thirds of the total billionaire population.[2] Overall, billionaire wealth has grown faster than the world economy, more than tripling from 2 percent to 7 percent of GDP between 1987 and 2012.

Why did we focus on self-made billionaires? Because creating a billion dollars or more in value is an incredible feat. If you have discipline and you work hard, you can become a top-notch accountant or a lawyer. Years of dedication and a little luck might propel you to partner status at PwC or a law firm, or perhaps into the C-suite at a Fortune 500 firm. Do that and you will likely achieve multimillionaire status, but your chances of becoming a billionaire along that path are almost zero. There are clear paths to wealth, but there is no tried-and-true road to megawealth. Billionaires have to do something extraordinary to make it as far as they do. Good luck plays a role, but luck will only allow a million-dollar idea to bring in a million dollars' worth of value. Becoming a billionaire requires luck *and* a great deal more.

Self-made billionaires thrive in an environment of shifting variables. Take Dietrich Mateschitz, the founder of Red Bull, who has generated cultish devotion for a drink that even devoted fans agree tastes like cough syrup. Or Sara Blakely, a fax saleswoman/stand-up comic, who had the all-too-common problem of visible panty lines under her white pants. Spanx, the hosiery company she created to make the product she wanted, earned accolades from self-made billionaire tastemaker Oprah Winfrey and generated explosive growth in an era when hosiery stalwarts were seeing their revenues plummet. Or Joe Mansueto, the soft-spoken founder of Morningstar, who at the age of twenty-three was forced to sift through dozens of mutual fund prospectuses in order to manage his fledgling personal investment portfolio. Surrounded by piles of paper, he thought, "Gee, this could be a business." Mateschitz, Blakely, Mansueto, and hundreds of others—these are the people creating hugely profitable businesses in today's world.

When we looked more closely at self-made billionaires, we found that sound judgment was not in short supply. These are people who have dealt with the world as it is, made excruciating choices, and placed bets based on hard realities. But what truly makes them stand out is that their judgment is balanced by extraordinary imaginative vision.

Cultivating a balance of judgment and vision is a challenging task. Findings from neuroscience suggest that for most people, judgment and imagination sit on opposite ends of a mental spectrum. The more skilled one is at seeing things as they are (judgment) the harder it is to see things as they might be (imagination).[3] But somehow, the population of self-made billionaires manages to defeat the binary mental spectrum that places judgment and imagination in opposition to each other.

The tactics and habits we identified that allow self-made billionaires to achieve that balance are the core of this book. They suggest practices that companies and individuals can adopt to enhance their value-creation capabilities.

So what is the source of the self-made billionaire effect? What allows them to create such massive value? How do they rise above the apparent trade-off between judgment and imagination? What other skills, habits, life experiences, or talents distinguish them from the pack? And most important, what can these insights teach us about the talent we as executives need to find and cultivate in order to thrive in challenging times?

We begin to answer these questions in Chapter 1, where we present our foundational findings on what makes self-made billionaires different from the average corporate executive. The findings not only surprised us, they also changed the way we think about executive talent and what we need to look for in the talent we bring into business and nurture.

1

EXPLODING MYTHS OF
EXTREME ENTREPRENEURSHIP

The test of a first-rate intelligence is the ability to hold
two opposed ideas in mind at the same time and still
retain the ability to function.
—F. SCOTT FITZGERALD

In 1984, Dietrich Mateschitz was a bored, forty-year-old marketing
executive at the German cosmetics company Blendax. He spent his
days peddling toothpaste and cosmetics to retailers around the world.
"All I could see was the same grey airplanes, the same grey suits, the
same grey faces. All the hotel bars looked the same, and so did the
women in them. I asked myself whether I wanted to spend the next
decade as I'd spent the previous one." [1] Then on a routine trip to Thailand—like dozens of others he had taken—Mateschitz had an insight
that would change his career.

While reading the newspaper one morning at his hotel, Mateschitz learned that the Japanese manufacturer of a line of supersweet
"health" drinks popular in Asia was the biggest taxpayer in Japan.

Mateschitz knew the drinks and had taken them for the energy boost they gave as an antidote to jet lag. There was nothing like them in the West. That they were a huge moneymaker had never occurred to Mateschitz, and he decided right then to quit his job and start a company to manufacture and market the drinks in Europe.

Within a few years, Red Bull, the business Mateschitz founded with Thai business associate Chaleo Yoovidhya—a toothpaste manufacturer who also had a sideline in beverages—had launched its signature carbonated beverage in Mateschitz's native Austria and in Slovenia. Within a decade Red Bull was in the UK, Germany, and eventually in the enormous beverage market in the United States. In all of the markets it entered, Red Bull became an almost overnight sensation. Red Bull was the first in what became, during the 1990s and 2000s, a burgeoning market of "energy" drinks, a beverage category that is neither a sports drink like Gatorade nor an amped-up soda like Mountain Dew. Red Bull charged through as a supersweet, caffeine-infused carbonated beverage that merged the appeal of sweet sodas and extreme sports into something entirely new: a drink that "gives you wings." Mateschitz redesigned the beverage to be a carbonated, less concentrated version of the syrupy shots he was inspired by, and he redesigned the traditional soda can as an eight-ounce bullet shape that signaled to the buyer that this was not just another cola.

Today, Red Bull is far more than the drink that carries its name. It is a media company; a Formula 1 franchise; a Nascar franchise; a sponsor of mountain climbers and skiers and other extreme sportsmen; a "philosophy," as its founder has said, of life lived in a heightened state of adrenaline-fused activity—all bred from the modest foundations of a good idea.[2]

HOW ARE BILLIONAIRES DIFFERENT?

The story of how Dietrich Mateschitz built his brand empire reads on the surface like many examples of extreme entrepreneurial success—there is the serendipitous moment of revelation, the useful connections to the right people, the willingness to risk his career on an uncertain venture. Yet not every insight, every business connection, every risk taken results in a billion dollars of value. That success is not evenly distributed across the range of good ideas made us ask the question that lies at the root of this book: namely, what enables self-made billionaires to create such massive value?

There are plenty of available truisms that get touted by thought leaders in response to that question. Extreme entrepreneurs take bigger risks, for example, or they focus on new markets. We didn't know at the outset whether any of these ideas were true, but on their own they didn't seem to explain the scale of success that these people achieve. Many people take risks, but very few reap high returns. Many entrepreneurs launch into new growth markets, but few emerge with a blockbuster hit.

The answer, we decided, was more complex. To find it, we first decided to dig deeper into the business literature to find what business scholars have to say from studying self-made billionaires. We expected to find a strong base of academic research focused on identifying the behaviors, characteristics, and secrets of success of self-made billionaires. What we found surprised us—in fact, no one had done a systematic study of self-made billionaires. We found plenty of isolated stories and first-person narratives culled from magazine profiles and autobiographies. But there have been only a few attempts at systematic evaluation of entrepreneurial success at any scale, and those evaluations often come to contradictory conclusions.[3]

Quickly it became clear that if we wanted answers, we would

need to look for them ourselves. Ultimately, that was a good thing—we didn't have to contend with prior research making strong conclusions that might influence our thinking.

We set up a research team in early 2012 at PwC, where Mitch is a vice chairman and John is the leader of Global Thought Leadership. To identify our research subjects, we took the 2012 *Forbes* list "The World's Billionaires" and eliminated people who had inherited their wealth from a parent, a spouse, or other family member. We also removed billionaires operating in markets that lack the regulatory transparency to ensure fair play—all billionaires take advantage of economic conditions, but we chose to focus on those operating in environments where reasonably transparent and competitive markets predominate.[4]

Left with roughly 600 people, we randomly selected 120, adjusted to mirror the geographic and industry distribution of the larger sample, and set out to learn as much as we could about them. We collected everything we could find that had been written about our subjects and captured biographical details (place of origin, age, marital status, family makeup) and the trajectory of their careers (When did they start their first business? What were some of the key inflection points in the growth of their primary business? At what point did they transition from modest entrepreneur to massive value creator?). Simultaneously, we invited a number of the people on our list to participate in interviews with us so we could learn more about them.

As we began collecting data and conducting interviews it became almost immediately clear that a lot of the truisms that get touted as the keys to successful entrepreneurship didn't stand up to the data we had. For instance:

▶ **Age**

Our tech-dominated era—populated by savvy wunder-kinder—has left the impression that most self-made billionaires cross that billion-dollar finish line early in their careers. While it is true that people like Bill Gates, Michael Dell, and Mark Zuckerberg made their first billion while still quite young—and with the first companies they formed—the majority of people in our sample are like Dietrich Mateschitz, who didn't hit the billion-dollar mark until well after his fortieth birthday. For more than 70 percent of the sample, the idea or transition that catapulted them to billion-dollar success happened after age thirty (see Figure 1-1).

Figure 1-1: Most Billionaires Are Already Mature Professionals When They Launch Their Blockbuster Idea

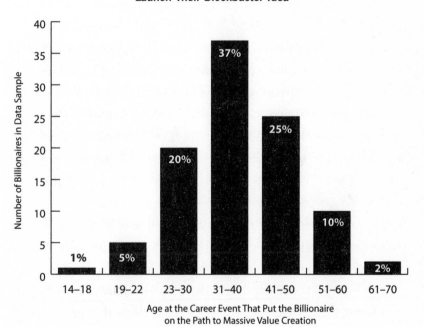

► **Industry**

Technology dominance has also led many to believe that the main path for self-made entrepreneurs is the tech sector, which is so often held up as a bastion of new wealth and meritocracy, where anyone with a great idea and the willingness to code for long hours can rise to the top. In fact, less than 20 percent of our sample of self-made billionaires came from tech. The money management and the consumer products industries are not far behind tech in terms of the number of self-made billionaires. Overall, more than nineteen different industries were represented in our sample, including oil and gas, apparel, food and beverages, publishing, printing, real estate development, entertainment, and hotels, *as well as* technology and tech services, among others.

▶ Greenfield Innovators

There is a general belief that self-made billionaires create "brand-new" things. To borrow a phrase from professors W. Chan Kim and Renée Mauborgne, of INSEAD, billionaires are believed to sail in "blue oceans." There's no question that exploring new market spaces has the potential to yield large profits, but it's not the route that most self-made billionaires chart. More than 80 percent of our sample of self-made billionaires earned their billions in red oceans—highly competitive, mature industries.

Dietrich Mateschitz again offers a case in point for this fact—he inserted Red Bull as a new product category (the "energy" drink) into an existing beverage market. He signaled its difference from existing drinks with both the skinny 8.4-ounce can and a premium price more than double that of a can of Coke. Such seemingly small tweaks may not seem as awesome as a new market innovation, but the value is still there.

▶ Luck

When we conducted a simple survey asking friends and colleagues about perceptions of self-made billionaires, we heard plenty of comments about "one-hit wonders" and a strong belief that many of the self-made have earned as much as they have because of luck. We could believe in luck if the majority of our sample had only one successful venture. But our data convinced us that luck alone does not explain the success of self-made billionaires, given that more than 90 percent of them have launched multiple successful businesses.

▶ **Exploitative Practices**

It's difficult to find any successful organization that hasn't been accused by someone, somewhere, of unsavory practices. Billionaires in particular are easy targets for such accusations. While we make no claims about their universal purity, as a group the businesses launched by the self-made billionaires in our sample lean toward the socially responsible end of the scale in their industries. Furthermore, a large number of self-made billionaires have signed the Giving Pledge, promising to give away more than half of their net worth; a significant portion are active in philanthropy or social projects.

▶ **Overnight Success**

It may seem that certain individuals form companies and suddenly enter the public consciousness with a meteorically successful product, but the reality is that many self-made billionaires reach extreme success only after many years of professional investment and commitment to a particular market space. They often exhibit early entrepreneurial drive: more than 50 percent had a first job before age eighteen; nearly 30 percent had launched their first entrepreneurial venture before age twenty-two; and almost 75 percent before age thirty (see Figure 1-2). Note that while some billionaires had the kind of humble upbringing that necessitated an early entry to work, they are in the minority—more than 75 percent of self-made billionaires were raised in households with affluence levels in the middle class or above.

Figure 1-2: Billionaires Start Early

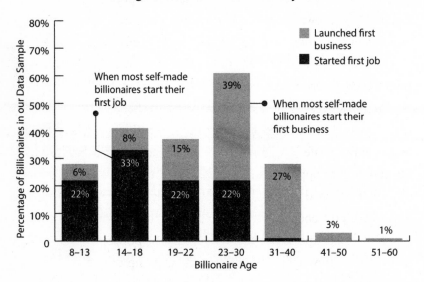

▶ Talent, but Also Practice

The billionaires' early ventures provided a great deal of practice in a couple of key areas, which improved any skills they already had. Seventy-five percent or more had direct sales experience; and almost 70 percent had ownership of a P&L before age thirty.

These are just a few of the counterintuitive findings that made it clear to us that there was a mismatch between what many claim to "know" about extreme success and what the data report.

PRODUCERS AND PERFORMERS

Left with a clean slate, we began searching for what is truly different about self-made billionaires. We looked at the data through the lens of our premise—that self-made billionaires approach the challenge of creating new value differently from most corporate managers and leaders. Somehow, self-made billionaires vault over the same obstacles to value creation that trip up the vast majority of executives.

We expected to find that self-made billionaires encountered a set of common *external* factors early in their lives—certain experiences or circumstances—that led them to act or behave in particularly driven ways. Maybe the majority had to contend with existential challenges early in life. Or they came from disadvantaged backgrounds. Or perhaps the opposite is true and most of them came from extraordinarily privileged homes. It became quickly apparent, however, that there were no trends in the data to suggest that a shared tenor of circumstances or experiences ran throughout the population. An equivalent number grew up extremely poor as grew up quite rich; an equal proportion failed to finish college as earned PhDs.

As we probed deeper, it became clear that the connection lay not in external circumstances but in what we have come to define as internal "habits of mind." Self-made billionaires are able to integrate ideas and actions that most individuals and organizations keep separate or even hold in direct tension to one another. We refer to this coexistence of forces as a duality. Self-made billionaires effectively operate in a world of dualities—they seamlessly hold on to multiple ideas, multiple perspectives, and multiple scales.[5]

These distinctive habits of mind that we observed in self-made billionaires play out in a variety of ways. We have already mentioned the ability to cultivate imagination—that ability to envision what could be—while maintaining judgment—the ability to see things as they are.

Similar dualities apply to the way these billionaires approach managing their time, executing a business idea, handling risk, and balancing the talent pool in their own organizations. These dual habits of mind and action enable them to function as what we term *Producers:* they envision something new, bring together the people and the resources to create it, and sell it to customers who didn't know they needed it.

In contrast, the modern corporation has evolved to separate many of these dualities into different functions, which are then run by talented people who excel at optimizing within known systems. We call these leaders *Performers.* Performers are often very good at what they do. But they are celebrated and elevated precisely because they perform so well in one arena. That single-minded talent for reaching otherworldly heights within a defined environment—so necessary in many aspects of business—reinforces function-driven systems that discourage the integrated habits of mind and action necessary for Producers.

The science fiction writer Thomas Disch once wrote that "creativeness is the ability to see relationships where none exist." In fact, it is part of human nature to look for relationships, but creating something brand-new requires that a person not only be able to see relationships but also be able to separate the real relationships from the false ones. In other words, not all ideas are good ones. Recognizing when you have gold and when you just have rocks requires an integrative approach. It's about seeing relationships that matter to customers and from there unveiling a new empathetic insight.

Integration is counterintuitive in many organizations. Decades of focusing on optimization and efficiency have led many to specialize in breaking down problems and forming functions to manage the separate parts. They elevate Performers to optimize and excel in those separate functions. Producers, by contrast, revel in bringing clashing elements together.

Operating in a world of dualities is not the same as managing competing demands such as "deliver on time and under budget" or "satisfy the customer and keep costs down." Corporations are constantly putting objectives in tension, creating challenges, and establishing stretch goals. But in most places it is clear that two requirements that seem to be in tension really aren't. The official corporate mandate may be to "do both" but everyone knows which metrics matter. If you hit quantifiable, short-term goals, the organization will support you.

A BATTLE AGAINST NATURE

The habits of mind and action that allow some individuals to thrive in a world of dualities come naturally to Producers, but they are not natural for the majority of the population gravitating toward the Performer end of the spectrum. There are a limited number of ideas or issues that most executives can attend to simultaneously. People can attempt to increase their "working memory," that system in the brain that allows us to hold on to multiple ideas or lines of thought, but it won't necessarily lead us to embrace duality. According to decades of psychological research, human beings do not generally like integrating opposing ideas. In fact, when confronted with ideas that challenge our core beliefs, we tend to discount or ignore them.

Yet we can overrule our inherent nature. Many of the self-made billionaires we studied appeared to be natural-born Producers, but the points noted above about the importance of practice and the long-term commitments that many of them make to the markets in which they eventually thrive show that they also need to hone and cultivate the habits of mind and action necessary to become fully developed Producers. Yes, inborn skill and abilities matter. But everyone—from the natural-born Producer to the gifted Performer—can build and hone the habits of mind that will make him or her a better manager, a better executive, a better entrepreneur, a more imaginative thinker, and a bigger value creator. And all businesses can build the organizational structures that support nascent Producers.

Think about running a marathon. There are a few people in the world with the natural athletic prowess, endurance, and pain tolerance to run with the professionals in a prestigious race like Boston, New York, or London. But the vast majority of healthy adults can finish a single marathon if they are willing to put in the time and effort. And even those who might not be able to run a full 26.2 miles can still achieve significant physical and mental improvement from the training regimen.

It's the same for the Producer's habits of mind and action. Not everyone will have and be able to execute a billion-dollar idea. But all of us can take steps to enable us to produce more value in what we do. The first step is to understand the habits of mind and develop them in ourselves, our team, and our organization. The following chapters will show you how to build practically on those habits and take action.

As highlighted in the opening passage of this chapter, a large number of self-made billionaires worked inside established organizations before they left to pursue their own ideas. Some viewed these jobs as way stations, places to learn from before they set out on their own. Many were fired, pushed out, or quit in a wave of frustration because their way of thinking and ideas were not recognized or valued. In all cases, the firms that employed them were not environments that supported creating massive value. And so Stephen Ross, Phil Knight, Joe Mansueto, George Soros, and dozens like them created massive new value by setting out on their own.

It doesn't have to be this way. Think about how many people have left your organization and gone on to create significant value elsewhere. What might have happened if they had stayed? Business leaders can learn to recognize emergent Producers, nurture their ideas, and create a space that allows them to develop and thrive *inside* the organization.

DUALITIES IN PRACTICE

Cultivating dual habits of mind starts with understanding the dualities that are most important. The five critical dualities we observed in the self-made billionaire population are:

▶ **Ideas—Empathetic Imagination**

Producers see blockbuster potential where others see only change. Their billion-dollar ideas come through the marriage of extreme empathy for the customer's needs and wants, and an imaginative mind-set that allows him or her to come up with and explore new, untested ideas.

▶ **Perspective—Patient Urgency**

Producers cannot predict the exact time to make an investment or bring a product to market, but they are willing to operate simultaneously at multiple speeds and time frames. They accept that timing is not under their control, and so they work fast, slow, super slow, or in all these modes at the same time. They urgently prepare to seize an opportunity but patiently wait for that opportunity to fully emerge.

▶ **Action—Inventive Execution**

Typical business practice tends to separate creative functions from the operational departments that bring ideas to market. Producers, on the other hand, approach execution of their ideas with the same integrative, inventive mind-set they applied to come up with a billion-dollar idea in the first place. Inventive freedom allows them to design aspects of the customer experience that others consider fixed, thus unlocking new value.

▶ Attitude—Taking a Relative View of Risk

Contrary to popular wisdom, self-made billionaires are not huge risk takers. But the risks they do worry about are much different from those most corporations focus on. They are not paralyzed by the absolute risk of losing an investment. Instead, their perceptions of risk are relative: they are far less concerned about losing what they have than of not being part of a bigger future. When they do experience setbacks— and many early Producer ventures produce only moderate results, or experience crippling setbacks—they have the resilience to try again.

▶ Leading—Leadership Partnership

The archetype of the solo genius is so pervasive in the way people talk about and think about extraordinary success that it obscures the real story of how good ideas become great businesses. The reality is that Producers are overwhelmingly *not* alone. Creating billions in value requires both a master Producer, who can bring together divergent ideas and resources into a blockbuster product design, and a virtuoso Performer, who can apply his or her creative acumen to optimizing the potential of that design. Thus, the Producer's most important duality, in fact, may not be self-contained: it is the partnership built between individuals with complementary skills and mutual trust.

Let's take a deeper look at this last duality—Leadership Partnership—because it seems to be in tension with the idea we introduced earlier about Producers exhibiting both active imagination and sound judgment. While it is true that Producers maintain a duality of judgment and imagination, they rarely have outlier skills in *both*. Think of Lynda and Stewart Resnick, the Producer-Performer pair behind Teleflora, POM Wonderful, and FIJI Water, in addition to various California agribusinesses. Stewart is strong on judgment—as Lynda put it, "He's the one who makes sure the businesses are profitable."[6] But converting the pomegranate from a West Coast health food store rarity into an expensive, mass-market drink required Lynda's imagination. She saw the long-term health-conscious antioxidant craze and she knew how to execute, attending to everything from the taste of the product to the shape of the bottle. Her genius not only moves millions of POM bottles a year but has also managed, within a matter of months, to rebrand a *fruit* and thus get millions of Americans to refer to clementines as "Cuties."

Many people with differing talents find themselves threatened by or in competition with one another, their opposing strengths creating a clash of worldviews. By contrast, the self-made billionaires we studied put a premium on the skills and perspectives of their complement. They have the confidence and insight to value the skills of the right partner who brings something necessary and distinct from what they have to offer.

HOW TO SHIFT THE BALANCE OF TALENT IN YOUR ORGANIZATION

Our research has opened our eyes to our own habits of mind and the myriad ways we inadvertently nudge ourselves and our colleagues to behave more like Performers. We have been pushing people to excel

in one area (that is, perform) instead of helping them to bring resources together in new ways to create new value (that is, produce).
We were convinced by listening to self-made billionaires reflect on the
frustration they felt as employees trapped inside existing organizations that leaders and organizations can and must change to encourage and capture Producer value.

Throughout the book we go into detail on several different ways
to change paths. First, organizations need to take actions that encourage all managers to develop Producer habits of mind. Right now the
range of talent in your organization resides on a Performer-Producer
continuum, the distribution of which resembles a bell curve tilted dramatically to the Performer side of the spectrum (see Figure 1-3).

Figure 1-3: The Standard Performer-Producer Distribution in Businesses

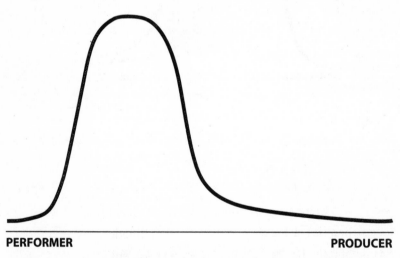

PERFORMER   **PRODUCER**

The steps we propose aim to shift the overall organizational profile incrementally from the Performer end toward the Producer end
(see Figure 1-4). Not everyone can be a Producer—this is not a value
judgment, it's an economic judgment. Performers play a critical and
necessary role in the organization, but they are not the ones creating

breakthrough value. Nonetheless, we believe that even the most die-hard Performers can benefit from cultivating in themselves and those around them some of the Producer habits of mind. Doing so is critical to thriving in our changeable world.

Figure 1-4: Shifting the Producer-Performer Distribution

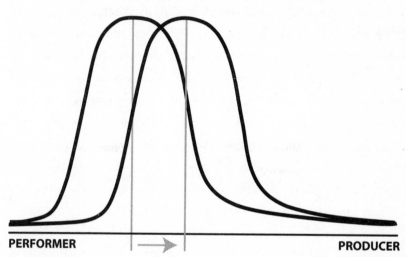

PERFORMER   PRODUCER

Producer talent and skill are nonetheless not evenly distributed and are not valuable or beneficial equally in every role in a corporation. While there are important and obvious benefits to having every manager practice a habit of mind like Empathetic Imagination, not everyone should be spending significant time engaged in Inventive Execution and attempting to change your business model. Even fewer should be adopting a full-on Producer mind-set that deals with risk.

We've organized the following chapters so that the number of people for whom the lessons apply decreases as you work through the ideas. This allows you to encourage each habit of mind for the appropriate people in the organization. As you get deeper into the book and begin to adopt these practices and policies, you will be able to better identify who in the organization has the Producer attributes and aptitudes necessary for further development. The prescriptive advice at the end of each chapter is geared toward making incremental improvements in your ability to create and capture new value.

We do not stop there. Incremental change is clearly not enough. Shifting a team of Performers is important but insufficient to meet the challenges that most organizations face. To excel, organizations need to find—and keep—at least a few exceptional Producers. That requires deeper cultural and organizational changes than we address in the final chapter. The conclusion lays out additional steps and approaches to transforming an organization in a way that will allow it to attract and retain world-class Producers. "Retaining" doesn't always mean that a world-class Producer will remain an employee of the organization. There are always going to be Producers who leave—that is the nature of the pure Producer type. By creating a Producer-friendly environment, however, you lay the groundwork for your organization to maintain a relationship with the Producers who pass through your hallways, and set up the potential for partnerships in the future. But that's a topic we'll address later. For now, let's take a look at what's to come in the rest of the book.

THE PRODUCER HABITS OF MIND

Throughout the following chapters we reveal how self-made billionaires bring scalable ideas to market through Producer qualities, with all the highs and lows along the way. We owe an enormous debt of gratitude to all of the people who were willing to meet with us in person. Their stories can help the rest of us develop the dual habits of mind we need to seize the opportunities that are all around us in these uncertain times.

The remainder of this book will explore the dualities, uncovered in our research, that enable self-made billionaires to create massive new value. We categorized them, respectively, as Idea, Perspective, Action, Attitude, and Leadership, and all the self-made billionaires we studied possess all of them, though any individual may be stronger in some categories than in others.

Chapter 2 explores where billion-dollar Producer **ideas** come from. We show how football franchise owner Jeffrey Lurie, financial publisher Joe Mansueto, sports apparel retailer Chip Wilson, serial entrepreneur Mark Cuban, and Chinese consumer goods entrepreneur Hui Lin Chit developed blockbuster ideas through *Empathetic Imagination,* a merging of deep practical insight into customer needs, with imaginative ideas.

Chapter 3 discusses the Producer perspective of **time and timing.** Producers like Steve Case, Groupon CEO Eric Lefkofsky, and real estate developer Alex Spanos bring the perspective of *Patient Urgency* to their work, unlike the typical corporate mind-set driven by quarters within a fiscal year. In the example of AOL, Steve Case spent ten years struggling to make money as he urgently built the network service provider and waited for the mass-market networked customer to emerge. Producers are patient about how long it will take for a major longitudinal trend to come to fruition but urgent about the need to have the capabilities, deals, and relationships in place when the customer is ready.

Chapter 4 discusses the process by which Producers take **action** to turn a good idea into a massively valuable reality. Pharmaceutical billionaire Michael Jaharis, cruising innovator Micky Arison, and hedge fund CEO Tom Steyer bring innovation to the process of execution. For them, every aspect of delivering a product is a candidate for innovation. They tackle product design, product delivery, pricing, business model, sales pitch, and in so doing they apply *Inventive Execution* to the process of bringing a product to market. This stands in stark contrast to most corporations, for which execution is inherited—the business model, pricing model, functions, sales pitch, and deal structure, nearly everything is treated as predefined by the models, costs, and pricing that already exist in the company and/or the industry. Producers are not constrained by these preexisting ideas.

Chapter 5 discusses the Producer's **attitude** toward risk. One finding from our research that surprised us is that the bravado that has come to be synonymous with entrepreneurial risk taking is in large part a myth. Through the successes, failures, and do-overs experienced by the real estate developer Stephen Ross, oil-and-gas entrepreneur T. Boone Pickens, Chinese paper products producer Yan Cheung, and others, we show how Producers adopt a *Relative View of Risk*. The *types* of risks they avoid are quite different from the ones that corporations traditionally endeavor to minimize. The result is that they pursue opportunities that others don't even see, resulting in massive value.

Chapter 6 discusses the Producer's **leadership** practice of partnering with a person whose talents and worldview contrast and complement his or her own. Most companies are hardwired to focus either on the individual or on teams. But Producers like John Paul DeJoria, founder of John Paul Mitchell Systems and Patrón Spirits, and mall developers Herb and Mel Simon demonstrate the varied ways in which Leadership Partnership—two individuals working together, complementing each other—uncovers efficiencies and creative ideas that outperform other options. Specifically, this chapter is about creating a duality by matching yourself with a partner who has conflicting but complementary skills.

The failed histories of so many Producers in corporate environments makes clear that we have some work to do to identify the

Producers in our midst and cultivate an environment in which they feel welcome and valued. The *Conclusion* explains specific areas where individual managers and whole organizations can develop in order to better identify, hire, hone, and retain more Producers. We also introduce examples taken from a variety of domains to show how certain process and management innovations can yield big benefits.

2

EMPATHETIC IMAGINATION:
The Art of Designing the Blockbuster

Inspiration exists, but it has to find us working.
—PABLO PICASSO

When a twenty-four-year-old Joe Mansueto began buying mutual funds in the early 1980s he was wading into lonely territory. Mutual funds had been around since before the Great Depression, but they were a niche product for a niche audience—only wealthy individuals invested in the stock market, and most of them used brokers who pushed individual stocks. Relatively few brokers promoted mutual funds, resulting in few individual investors' buying them.

None of this deterred Mansueto. A meticulous person, he was unintimidated by the effort required to contact multiple mutual fund companies and order the quarterly prospectuses for each fund he wanted to follow. They came in the mail, pounds of paper delivered to the front step, which Mansueto then lugged up to his one-bedroom apartment to pore over at the kitchen table. It was during one research session that he thought to himself how useful it would be if someone compiled a report that gave all the information about comparable funds in a simple, attractive format, with a quick assessment that compared funds on the basis of certain features. "Gee, this could be a business," he recalled thinking.

Two years later—after brief stints learning about the financial sector at an investment bank and a financial management firm—Mansueto launched Morningstar, a business that specializes in investment research, with a particular focus on mutual fund performance. Over the subsequent thirty years, mutual funds in the United States went from a niche product to a mainstream investment tool with more than eight thousand available options and $2.8 trillion invested. Morningstar was able to ride that growth, offering a product of such obvious value to the mainstream investor that it is hard to imagine there was ever a time when people operated without it. The business expanded exponentially from 1984, when Mansueto penned the first edition of his flagship *Mutual Fund Sourcebook,* to its present status as a multicountry, multiproduct financial publishing firm.[1]

THE DUAL POWER OF EMPATHIC INSIGHT AND IMAGINATION

In the example of how Joe Mansueto conceived his business we see a set of dynamics that occur throughout the billionaire population. There is a market on the brink of change; an untapped, unrecognized need about to be unleashed; and a Producer with deep empathy about the needs of the customer, coupled with the imagination to convert that empathetic insight into a great business idea with broad market potential. The dual power of empathetic insight and imagination is the Producer's formula for conceiving the blockbuster idea.

It's easy to see in hindsight what makes the blockbuster unique and innovative. Billion-dollar businesses often share an element of ex post facto obviousness that belies the fact that many Producers experience almost crippling resistance to their ideas in the early months and years of their ventures. People who genuinely know the markets these Producers are trying to penetrate argue that their ideas won't fly. For example, Sara Blakely, the founder of Spanx, struggled to find a hosiery factory willing to create prototypes for her because the factory owners believed her idea of footless, slimming tights was destined for failure in a struggling market in which old stalwarts like L'eggs and Hanes were losing revenue.

These examples should make clear that good ideas are hard to find, and great ideas even harder. But they are conceivable by Producers who consciously and meticulously cultivate the skills of empathy and creativity in order to see potential where others don't.

What allows Producers to see what others cannot? What allows them to merge empathic insight with imagination? Where do their blockbuster ideas come from?

Our research shows that Producers generate ideas through a mode of creativity known as divergent thinking. Divergent thinking involves the free flow of different ideas and associations for the purpose of identifying solutions to a problem. Everyone at the strategic levels of business must engage in some divergent thinking. The difference in the quality—or, rather, the imaginativeness—of the outputs depends on the quality and variety of the inputs and the *relative emphasis* the Producer places on imagining what could be and judging it based on what already exists. Imaginative people are able to do both with near simultaneity—they can imagine new ideas and evaluate how the idea can be improved and enhanced.[2]

This is markedly different from how most of us operate in business circles. Nature works against most of us by isolating our imaginative impulses from our evaluative capabilities. Then nurture kicks in, and through culture or training or fear we learn to tamp down our imaginations and focus instead on ideas that feel comfortable and attainable. As a result, when it comes to developing new ideas we don't allow ourselves the space to ask that "what if" question in a truly open-ended way. We put boundaries around our thinking before we have even begun. We say, for example, that our ideas have to serve the customers we already have, or be executed using techniques we already know how to use, or earn a certain amount of revenue within twelve months. We thus develop and present only those ideas we believe decision makers will accept, or that fit into the existing market or strategic goals, or that we have the infrastructure and skills to execute. By definition these ideas are incremental. Incremental improvement is fine when cultivated as a stepping-stone to exponential change. But in so many businesses incremental is as far as it goes, and is unlikely to produce a breakthrough.

True Producers don't operate that way. They don't shut down an idea just because it is outrageous or improbable or hard to execute. They are capable of full imaginative ideation, developed over a lifetime of honing expertise, cultivating curiosity, and empathizing with the customer. As a result, they are able to escape automatic modes of thinking and have insights capable of creating explosive value.

EXPERTISE AND THE IMAGINATION

Jeffrey Lurie, the billionaire owner of the Philadelphia Eagles, had always been an avid sports fan. Football, basketball, baseball, hockey—he'd watched all of them live and on television while growing up in Boston. But when it was time to start a career, he went into the family business as an executive with General Cinema, the movie theater chain his grandfather founded. Lurie acted as a liaison between the family business and Hollywood studios, and after a few years he launched a production company of his own, Harcourt, where he produced a handful of films, both for theater distribution and for television.[3] By almost any measure he was a success, and one of his films, *Inside Job,* went on to win an Academy Award.

Despite his success, in the early 1990s Lurie began to feel that he'd been looking for blockbuster hits in the wrong place. "It dawned on me that there was a real separation in those days between the movie/television business and the sports business," he said when we sat down with him at his spacious, windowed office overlooking the Eagles' practice fields. "There was almost no connection. Nobody really saw the fact that the NFL was producing hit television shows that were starting to dwarf anything that Hollywood was producing. The marketplace was valuing television production in a very, very strong way. Yet there was no real value for guaranteed hit-making [like NFL games provided]. So that combined with the notion that—I think several of us kind of realized—the distribution of this was just beginning. It wasn't just going to be NBC, CBS, ABC, and a couple of pay cable channels, HBO and Showtime, which is what it was in those days. You started to see satellite. You started to see cable. It was before the Internet, so nobody anticipated exactly how that was going to play out. I felt there was going to be a significant paradigm shift."

Like many blockbuster ideas, it is obvious now, in our reality TV era, that consumers would embrace sports as a form of entertainment, and that sports programming would therefore be priced competitively with, say, *Homeland.* In fact, Lurie's insight has become so fully dominant in today's sports world that sports coaches regularly refer to what they do as part of the entertainment business. But Lurie repeatedly asserted during our conversation that his initial insight into the future of football as entertainment was not obvious from the start.

The record supports his assertion. The $185 million purchase price that Lurie ultimately negotiated with then–Eagles owner Norman Braman in early 1994 was the highest price ever paid for an NFL franchise, so high that even Lurie himself had a moment of concern when the deal was done and he finally got a clear look at what he had bought, complete with run-down practice facilities and a dilapidated stadium. "I get here and I look at the facilities and I'm thinking, 'I just bought this? Sight unseen?' Rats are running across the office I'm in. No windows. People were like, 'Who is this young kid?'"

That same day, the *Wall Street Journal* published an article critical of Braman's tenure over the Eagles, and of Lurie's purchase, which the author characterized as an emotional, juvenile buy with a purchase price that far exceeded the value of the team.[4]

"And the worst part of it," Lurie said of his reaction to the *WSJ* piece, "was that I thought, 'I think they're right. I just wired a hundred and eighty-five million dollars to Norman Braman. He really must have taken me. I don't know what I'm doing and they do and I might be really dumb here." It was too late by then, and Lurie is not one to mope. In any event, those feelings were fleeting. He was sure of his insight that the worlds of sports and entertainment were going to merge and that his job, after acquiring the team, was to revitalize the Eagles into a world-class franchise capable of inspiring what is known throughout the United States as a loyal and passionate Philadelphia fan base. "I just sort of ate those words and said, 'Okay. I'm going to plow ahead and do everything I planned and see what happens.'"

He didn't have to wait long for affirmation of his vision. "Right after I bought the team, the Glazers bought Tampa Bay for the same or more, and that's when Fox [Broadcasting] got in the game. That was the game-changer. A new network game-changer."

All Oceans Are Purple

When we started researching the evolution of self-made billionaires and their businesses, we had some clichéd expectations about business inspiration as a magical, accidental—even lucky—process. Some of the language the billionaires used to describe their experiences conformed at first to this viewpoint. Jeffrey Lurie told us, "It was a sort of an 'a-ha' moment. It wasn't some long figuring out, some long analytical process. It was a paradigm change. Entertainment could come from anywhere. Blockbuster ratings and demand to see could come from anything."

Lurie's experience could be more accurately characterized as an "a-ha" moment forty years in the making—the approximate age Lurie was when he bought the team, and the amount of time it took him to amass the knowledge and expertise he needed to realize the opportunity and act on it. In reality, blockbuster ideation is more accurately defined as cumulative and iterative. When we look at the circumstances through which so many self-made billionaires come up with the idea that snowballs into a blockbuster, we don't see a random and instantaneous flash out of nowhere, but instead a deliberate accumulation of knowledge and experience acquired through a long-term commitment to a particular domain. Though there are some exceptions, the blockbuster idea is most often steeped in a set of skills or ideas that the billionaire has been immersed in for years—sometimes even decades.

Joe Mansueto was a very young man when he had the idea that would eventually become Morningstar, but he was already a serial entrepreneur and more experienced than most in the art of investing—he had been managing his own growing portfolio for years, and had developed such a reputation for smart, profitable investing that other members of his family had given him their money to manage for them. Nor was Jeffrey Lurie's ability to see an entertainment paradigm shift an accident of proximity. He could visualize it so exactly because he was so deeply entrenched in the workings of the film industry and had an obsessive love of spectator sports.

The role that experience plays in imagining the blockbuster hit may explain where billionaires tend to launch their businesses. Ask any man on the street to list five self-made billionaires, regardless of whether the street is in New York, Shanghai, Mumbai, London, or Mexico City, and we bet that at least three out of five will be billionaires who earned their money in the technology, telecommunications, or media sectors. Steve Jobs and Bill Gates might show up on the list, as might Alibaba's Jack Ma, Foxconn's Terry Gou, Mexican telecommunications magnate Carlos Slim, Google's Larry Page and Sergey Brin, Bharti Airtel founder Sunil Mittal, and worldwide personality and media maven Oprah Winfrey. Billionaires who reach celebrity status tend to be associated with new industries or stunning innovations, so much so that when professionals talk about extreme success or wealth they tend to associate it with the discovery of entirely new sectors, such as the emergent PC market or the explosion of the Internet.

The INSEAD academics Renée Mauborgne and W. Chan Kim dubbed these new spaces "Blue Oceans" in their highly regarded book, *Blue Ocean Strategy*. "Blue Oceans" offers an emotive and useful metaphor for the belief that companies need to look for brand-new territory in order to create huge value, while "Red Oceans"—those bloody, battle-ridden markets challenged by a large number of competitors—are tapped out.

While Mauborgne and Kim captured the way that corporations tend to think about untapped markets, Producers do not appear to be concerned with these distinctions. From the outside, the markets they work in all look purple, a blending of new approaches within old modes that reveal ways to re-create the space. James Dyson didn't stop reimagining the vacuum cleaner because Mr. Hoover got there first. He just imagined it better, as a more beautiful object created for a public trained by brands like Braun and Apple to *want* to see function in the form.

In fact, 80 percent of the self-made billionaires we studied made their fortunes in contested market spaces that would by any measure be considered "red." Billionaires don't seem to view the world that way, however. To them, all oceans are purple, a blending of available opportunity extant within established practice. John Paul DeJoria launched John Paul Mitchell Systems into the populated market of high-end hair care; there were other ways to pay sellers online before Elon Musk bought PayPal; Bharti Enterprises founder Sunil Mittal got his start importing *known,* legacy technologies into India; Sara Blakely's Spanx were inserted into a hosiery market dominated by L'eggs and Hanes; Carnival Cruise billionaire Micky Arison made his billions by reinventing the cruising business away from its status as a vacation option only for the wealthy and elderly; James Dyson invented the dual cyclone to compete in a product space that was so entrenched that Mr. Hoover's name had become synonymous with "vacuum cleaner"; Farallon hedge fund founder Tom Steyer employed investing techniques similar to his peers; the housing developer Eli Broad embraced his flagship idea of building affordable homes without basements in part because he saw it had already been done somewhere else; coffee was already thousands of years old—one of the oldest commodities in the world—when Howard Schultz bought and then revamped Starbucks; and Glen Taylor, whose business was a printing shop, was part of a wave of business owners recognizing the escalating investments people were making in weddings.

These examples are great news for established corporations: they make clear that the opportunities are there, all the time, to create a blockbuster product within an existing market. The Producers in your midst understand that nothing is permanent and no market is owned solely by a single product or idea. Those who can take advantage of the flux can win big.

Producers constantly take on and reinvent products or approaches in established markets. From this act of imagination they often emerge with a blockbuster play. Their deep knowledge about a certain status quo in their industries consistently allows them to see the potential for change in the making—to make out veins of purple. On closer reflection, the story of the upstart newcomer or the overnight sensation that is so popular in our Internet era is more likely to have a knowledgeable veteran at the helm, someone who understands how things are usually done and has enough imagination to envision an alternative.

"I had seen this movie before"

Chip Wilson, the founder of Lululemon, illustrates the role that knowledge and immersion played in his ability to see a blockbuster business in the ancient practice of yoga.

The first thing we noticed when we met with Wilson in Australia was his size—six foot three with the broad shoulders of the Canadian junior national butterfly champion he was as a kid. Sports were at the center of the conversation when he was growing up—sports and *clothes*. His dad was a phys-ed teacher and his mom was a sewing hobbyist, so when Wilson wasn't outside with his dad or at the pool practicing, he sat with his mom at the sewing machine. "I probably got my ten thousand hours," he said to us of the experience.[5]

The California-born billionaire grew up in Vancouver, Canada, returning stateside for a month every summer during his childhood to visit his grandparents. The surfing craze was just starting in California's beach towns when Wilson was a teenager, and he joined in when he could, taking a break when he was nineteen to go with a friend to Alaska to work on the oil pipeline. He returned home after a year with what was—for a twenty-year-old with no obligations—a small fortune. He was self-sufficient, able to put himself through college, and take trips to Europe and Asia.

The knowledge Wilson had gained about fabrics, clothing construction, and international fashion started to bear fruit. "There were surf shorts," he said, "but in those days, I mean, really you could tell the year of a dime in your pocket, the shorts were so tight. I was a big guy, so for me to actually wear stuff I had to make it."

Wilson started making clothes for other people. The styles he saw in California weren't available in Vancouver, so he first made a woman's short inspired by one he'd bought in the United States as a gift for his girlfriend. Then, as he got more into surfing, he decided that a longer, looser short would work better for surfers than the tight shorts that were in style, so he made some of those too. With two products he approached the major Canadian department stores Eaton's and The Bay, but they weren't interested, so he set up his own store, Westbeach Surf, with $10,000 of start-up capital he'd earned on the pipeline.

"No one had ever made those before," he said of the baggier, longer shorts he designed. "I sold a couple of million of them. Basically, I took the surf industry. I was the first one to take it into Europe and then I took it to Japan. And then when skateboarding hit that was the perfect short for skateboarding. . . . And I was just perfectly situated in Vancouver. Windsor Mountain was there and it had a glacier and all the fourteen- and fifteen-year-olds in the world came to Windsor during the summertime to snowboard. So I thought, 'Now there's something I can be very authentic at and really understand,' and I could see the [snowboarding] market ten years before anybody."

Many billionaire businesses experience years of slow growth, mediocre outputs, and even outright failures. Just as Picasso produced literally thousands of paintings in his lifetime, but only a handful of true masterpieces, 94 percent of the billionaires in our sample have created or led more than one business, but not all of the businesses generated a billion dollars in value. Having a blockbuster idea requires real immersion in a subject, real willingness to come up with many ideas, and the ability to suspend judgment of ideas that may seem odd or out there and to take chances and potentially fail.

In the case of Chip Wilson, he had no exceptional immunity to making the wrong call. "I had a couple of failures in there," he told us. "Beach volleyball didn't go anywhere, mountain biking didn't go anywhere. So, it's not like I could see every trend go through."

But he definitely saw enough with Westbeach to know what would win and when he should get out. Wilson sold the company, then Westbeach Snowboard, Ltd., in 1997, just as it was beginning to struggle—Westbeach sold 70 percent of its products in Japan, according to Wilson, so when Japan began its economic malaise of the 1990s, Westbeach was deeply affected. But it wasn't long before Wilson saw what his next step was going to be.

"When I saw yoga the feeling that I got out of it was the same feeling out of surf, skate, and snowboarding. And I could tell: I had expertise in technical clothing and I saw a class go from six to thirty people in thirty days—and I had seen this movie before."

In 1998, Wilson launched Lululemon, the yoga clothing retailer that established yoga chic, made one of the first comfortable, stylish flat seam workout pants on the market, and turned Wilson into a billionaire. Far from an a-ha moment of miraculous inspiration, Lululemon was a natural offshoot of Wilson's talent and experience of more than twenty years. Because he knew so much about clothing, sports, and the international spread of sport trends, he was able to build a billion-dollar business to capitalize on the yoga trend.

CURIOSITY

Experience counts for a lot in generating practically creative ideas, but experience might bring little benefit without a sense of natural curiosity, that impulse to ask "why" companies or markets operate a certain way, or "what if" about new, seemingly strange ideas. In our

research we observed a direct connection between a habit of
in the billionaire population and the discovery of an idea that create
a billion-dollar business.

This observation gels with another finding from psychology and
neuroscience literature, namely that creative people are more likely to
exhibit what psychologists refer to as openness to experience. Openness to experience is one of the "Big Five" personality traits that psychologists use as a framework to define an individual's personality
"type." Openness to experience is marked by a sense of curiosity and
adventurousness, a willingness to explore and learn about people,
places, ideas, cultures, and other aspects of life that are outside one's
immediate experience.[6]

Reading was the most popular method used by billionaires to get
inspiration. The billionaire home builder Eli Broad, for example, read
multiple newspapers every day when he was a twenty-year-old accountant. It was the 1950s and the postwar baby boom was under
way and a subject of heated discussion in the news. Broad's reading
habit catalyzed his imagination and he started thinking about twenty-
year-olds of the future and how the changing demographics of the
United States would create burgeoning demand for affordable homes
for young up-and-comers. This empathetic insight into the wants and
needs of the baby boom generation allowed him to imagine an affordable home-building business, which he honed and refined with his
partner, Don Kaufman, an experienced home builder who happened
to be a family member (Kaufman was married to a cousin of Broad's
wife). Together, the two created a new firm designed to capitalize on
the opportunity.[7]

We told the story in Chapter 1 of how Dietrich Mateschitz, the
founder of Red Bull, likewise got the idea to start an energy drink
business from reading about the owner of a brand of syrupy energy
drink in the newspaper. Mateschitz was working at the time for
Blendax, the German cosmetics firm. He frequently traveled to Asia

on business, and he was familiar with the drinks—he had even used one brand to good effect as a tool against jet lag. But he hadn't considered their commercial potential until he read in *Newsweek* about the Japanese manufacturer of the drinks.[8] Mateschitz concluded that the drinks were big moneymakers, a fact that by itself would have led to nothing if Mateschitz had not taken it a step further to consider whether a Western consumer would embrace them. His empathetic insight into the needs of active, outdoorsy consumers convinced him that there was a market in the West for a diluted, carbonated energy drink, and he started the wheels rolling on a business to create just that.

Then there is the serial entrepreneur Mark Cuban, currently the owner of the Dallas Mavericks, who credits his appetite for information as the source of his success. Cuban's habit of getting as much information as he can dates back to when he was a kid trading stamps and baseball cards. Even then his curiosity helped him gain an edge over other buyers.

"I remember staying up till three, four, or five in the morning reading about stamps," he told us when we spoke with him at his offices in Dallas. "I memorized the value of everything so that when I went to a stamp shop, I'd know. I learned early on that most people don't do the work and that if I was prepared, I would have an edge. It was same with baseball cards. What was the demand for baseball cards? I probably was ten and there's a park down the street where I grew up and I would repackage baseball cards that I bought and go down there and I could charge a premium. I was doing the math so I could make money. I just think I was wired that way."[9]

This habit served him well over the years when the transactions started to get larger and more serious. Cuban formed MicroSolutions in the mid-1980s to service the burgeoning population of business computer users. "I was still just ten months from my first introduction to PCs, and had no clue about multi-user systems," he has written about his first days in business. He learned what he needed to know by taking the time *to read* about it. "I read every book and magazine I could. One good idea would lead to a customer or a solution, and those magazines and books paid for themselves many times over."[10]

Billionaires use other methods to satisfy their curiosity. Some, like Steve Jobs of Apple or Steve Case of AOL, went to liberal arts schools that encouraged cross-disciplinary study. When Case reflected on his experience at Williams College, consistently ranked among the top three liberal arts colleges in the United States, he described the environment as a kind of laboratory for imaginative thinking. "Liberal arts education is important," Case told us, "particularly in a world that's changing rapidly, because there's a lot of fluidity. There's the melding of different perspectives, having a sense of things and having a sense of how to learn about things and to look for connections. How do you connect the dots between disparate thoughts? It was more about appreciating the value of learning and understanding that it was the ability to take this information and dissect it and reconnect it. Like a Lego, how do you take all these pieces on a table and then reassemble them in interesting ways?"

Lastly, we saw those billionaires with particularly extrovert personalities sate their curiosity through social learning. One oft-repeated story about Jack Ma, the founder of Alibaba, the largest e-commerce site in Asia, tells of how he used to ride his bicycle every day to the hotel in his city to offer guided tours to the Western businesspeople staying there. Ma got to practice his English and ask a lot of questions about what the visitors liked about working in China. That experience helped him see the potential for systems that could make commerce easier, like China Pages, a service he created to host Web pages for Chinese businesses, and later at Alibaba with its multiple e-commerce business platforms enabling B2B, B2C, and C2C transactions.

PRACTICING EMPATHY

We've pointed out multiple times in this chapter that blockbuster ideation begins with empathy—an insight, honed over years or decades of experience in a market, into what potential customers, value chain partners, or investors are going to embrace. The ability to empathize captures the intuitive nature, the "felt sense" as Jeffrey Lurie called it in our interview with him, of what masses of people are going to want from a product that does not yet exist. By definition, blockbuster ideas appeal to huge numbers of people, customers in large markets or participants in major long-term trends. In the nuances of the product itself and its delivery—which we discuss in Chapter 4—billionaires capitalize on an unmet market need.

Steve Case, the founder of AOL, had his own empathetic insight in the early years he spent building the online content provider. AOL is often spoken of as an "overnight success" of the Internet era, but in fact Case and his team had been building the company for ten years before it became a known player. In its early years before the explosion of the Internet, AOL provided dial-up connections to a closed, proprietary communication network. Competitors like CompuServe started with similar products but were geared to technology professionals and other tech-savvy communities, and as a result, the functionality and interface were developed for that smaller, though active, audience.[11]

Case had a different take—he believed that online communication was a major trend for everyone, that it would become the mass-market system it is today. The market clearly didn't exist yet, but Case did not compromise on his vision. Instead, his vision drove AOL to target its product to the mass market, a decision that led to significant investments in streamlining the sign-up and connection processes, reducing the functionality, creating a highly usable, attractive (for the time) user interface, and, later, marketing to every household in America by sending free sign-up CDs through the mail and launching an unlimited data-pricing model that initially taxed the system. The tech community may have initially ignored AOL, but Case's empathetic insight into what the average user would need brought the company much further into the future.

Such empathetic insight is intimately linked to deep experiential knowledge—these Producers know the customers, but more important, they know what those customers will embrace today and have a strong sense of what they will need in the future.

We can see this play out through a number of iterations for those billionaires whose businesses evolved and shifted focus over time, as it did for Hengan International billionaire Hui Lin Chit.[12] Mr. Chit was a young village farmer in the region of Anhui, China, in the 1970s when China began the economic reform program that allowed private individuals to start their own businesses. "[I started] a zipper factory that was very small and did not need a lot of capital," Mr. Chit told us when we met with him at his offices in Anhai. "The machine [used to make zippers] was very simple, with a manual process and did not need much investment." But the low cost of entry to the zipper business made it easy for others to get involved as well. "More and more families started their own zipper business since the barrier of entry was low. We made less and less, and I sensed there was no future in it."

Still, there were plenty of other products needed in the country, and plenty of room for competitive growth. Mr. Chit expanded into apparel, also on a small scale: "My neighbors brought sewing machines to my house. We drew the style and they did the sewing." He also helped a publishing company with its shipping processes. He continued in this way, starting and expanding different lines until a friend told him about sanitary napkins. The machine needed to manufacture them cost $80,000, Mr. Chit told us—too much for him to invest on his own. So he partnered with Sze Man Bok, another entrepreneur in the garment business, and started what would become Hengan International to manufacture sanitary napkins.

Hengan targeted lower-income women in the villages with a product that was far superior, cleaner, and safer than the self-made alternatives so many poor women used at the time. Even when Procter & Gamble (P&G) entered the Chinese market in 1985 with a line of feminine products made and priced for wealthy, urban women, Hengan continued its focus on the average citizen and gradually grew in production and quality. Over time, it expanded upmarket so that in 1992 it launched a line of feminine products in direct competition with P&G's. Hengan has since launched other products, such as tissues, its largest product category, and disposable diapers. Today Hengan is China's largest domestic manufacturer of these products.

Empathy drove so many of the business lines Mr. Chit pursued. "Some people ask me why I do not enter other markets with higher profits, such as property development," Mr. Chit said to us. "I did not because I do not think that I understand that market. I believe in the consumer market, which is a continuing growth market in China. If we focus on this area and pay more attention to innovate the products, we will continue to grow."

BLOCKBUSTERS COME FROM EMPATHETIC INSIGHTS ABOUT TODAY AND TOMORROW

Hui Lin Chit's focus on understanding a market, and the customers, may not sound, on the surface, remarkably different from the ways that many business executives talk about the need to "know the market" or "put the customer first." The difference lies in the translation. Established businesses are so occupied by day-to-day operations that many are challenged to take the knowledge they have of how the customer behaves today and translate it into a future vision for a breakthrough product. The story we told earlier in this chapter of how Sara Blakely almost failed in her attempts to launch Spanx illustrates this form of tunnel vision.

But Blakely, a stand-up comic supporting herself as an office supplies saleswoman, had firsthand empathetic insight into what young, fashion-forward women need to feel good in their clothes. Spanx in many ways was built to produce the product that Blakely herself wanted. The idea came to her one night before a stand-up performance. As she was getting dressed, she pulled a pair of white pants out of her closet. She'd bought them years before but never worn them because she didn't like the way her underwear showed through the light fabric. For some reason that day she decided to take a pair of nude pantyhose from her underwear drawer, cut the feet off, and pull them on to wear under her pants. The effect was exactly what she wanted—the pantyhose smoothed the line of her clothes while remaining invisible under them.

She knew she was onto something and started putting the pieces in motion to start a business. Then she hit a glitch with the manufacturers. She contacted more than one hundred hosiery factories in the United States, and they all turned her down. These manufacturers should have been the first with insights into the needs of the customer, but they were using indirect data about the slipping numbers in the hosiery market to determine the value of a new idea. Blakely's luck changed only when one of the factory owners who had originally rejected her idea agreed to a trial run. What caused his change of heart? He reportedly went home after work and over dinner told his teenage daughters about Blakely. "We want those," they said.[13] Seeing the response of the real target audience made him change his mind about the potential for Spanx, and a billion-dollar business was born.

How many of us have found ourselves in a similar situation to those dozens of hosiery manufacturers, having rejected a great idea only to find, later, that someone else or another organization made a success of it?

SERVING THE CUSTOMER, NOT THE COMPETENCY

It is reassuring—even exciting—to see how billionaires insert new ideas into competitive markets. It's also worth considering the ways in which established firms get it wrong. Part of the issue may lie in the tendency—almost ubiquitous and completely understandable—to emphasize in-house competencies over the evolving needs of the customer. Management gurus C. K. Prahalad and Gary Hamel were railing against a certain lack of corporate focus when they published "Core Competence of the Corporation" in the *Harvard Business Review* in 1990.[14] But focusing on the competencies of today is exactly what causes companies to get stuck in the markets they serve and the products they deliver *now,* with little eye for the shifts and innovations they will need for tomorrow. Sometimes it takes a slight twist in perspective to see opportunities through a different lens.

Glen Taylor, the billionaire founder of the Taylor Corporation, was a junior employee at Carlson Letter Service, a local printing company, when he had the empathetic insight that allowed him to turn the business into the leader in wedding merchandise. Taylor was a Minnesota farm boy studying math and physics at Minnesota State when he started a part-time job with Carlson. Taylor intended to work for Mr. Carlson until he finished his studies and became a teacher. But when Taylor was set to graduate, Mr. Carlson offered him a full-time job, along with an implied promise that Taylor would take over when he retired. Still, Taylor wasn't convinced.[15]

"You don't really have a business here," Taylor recalled telling his boss. "It is just not a business. We don't have a product or anything like that." When Mr. Carlson asked Taylor what he thought could be the company's product, he said, "Maybe our product could be wedding stationery."

Why wedding stationery? "It was really the only thing that I thought he was making money on," Taylor told us when we met with him in his offices in Minnesota.

It seems a brash comment for a junior employee to make to his boss, but Taylor had by then already earned the trust of Mr. Carlson. He had the man's ear, earned by doing what Producers do—making connections and seeing opportunities that others ignore.

He operated that way right from the beginning. Growing up on a farm, Taylor came to the job at Carlson's with the mentality that you always need to fix a broken machine or system yourself, and upgrade how you work to get more from less. "If you don't have any money— and we didn't have any money—when things broke down you had to fix it," Taylor said of his upbringing.

Taylor didn't just fix the presses in Carlson's shop—he improved them. Within weeks on the job he got Mr. Carlson's attention for working twice as fast as anyone had before on the stamping press, a hated job that "no one wanted to do because it was a manual press you had to hold down." But Taylor didn't mind because he could make adjustments to the press and build a jig for it to make the job go faster, a change "no one had ever thought to do because you didn't get paid by the piece."

Soon Taylor could run the stamping press and another press simultaneously, a feat that earned him a lot of credibility and a promotion to work on stocks. "Now all of a sudden I was starting to work with Mr. Carlson a little differently," Taylor told us. "Working the stock and keeping track of inventory, I started to give him suggestions on how we could save money. 'Why don't you do this? They charge us extra, the freight is too much. I just looked at the bill. We should be ordering double and we could pay the same freight.' You know, just the little things like that."

By the time Mr. Carlson offered Taylor a full-time job, he had moved his young employee to purchasing, where Taylor's ability to see growth opportunities became even stronger. "We were a job shop. We did wedding stationery and we did invoices and we did envelopes, whatever anyone came in with we did. [Mr. Carlson] had never looked at which products made money, but being in purchasing it was pretty easy for me to figure out if something was making money or not."

Taylor's insight that wedding stationery was the company's sole source of profit sparked his imaginative vision to see the printing business not as an end in itself, but as a platform from which he could capitalize on the burgeoning growth in weddings and other special occasions. As a first step, he had the empathetic insight to know that if he made it easy for people to buy wedding invitations he could grow his best product far beyond stationery. With Mr. Carlson's permission, Taylor started courting clients by ordering phone books for the suburbs of St. Paul and Minneapolis and sending free samples of Carlson stationery to every retail store that advertised wedding invitations. "I did the same thing with the Dakotas, and Kansas. I put a little marketing thing together." He then worked to ensure his samples stood out from those of his competitors. Taylor went out and asked his friends (and friends of friends) what they wanted in their wedding stationery. "They said, 'I want stationery that matches my dress.' Or, 'I want something pretty on it other than just two rings intertwined.' So I went out and developed those products that the bride said she wanted."

It is easy in retrospect to say that what Taylor did to grow Carlson Letter Service was obvious, but those with deep knowledge and understanding of the market were not initially supportive of the idea. Mr. Carlson himself, a traditionalist in the printing industry, did not always understand what his employee was doing.

Taylor recalled, "I had the idea—I got some help from Hallmark— of having a groom in his tuxedo with a little red wagon and a little bride he is pulling. Mr. Carlson saw it and said, 'Who's going to buy that junk?' But I could see: brides at different locations in the country want different things." Taylor had the empathy to see what other people might buy. He also understood that wedding invitations represented just the entry point from which the bride and groom could be steered to any number of add-on, complementary products. Within months the shop's wedding stationery business was exploding. Taylor grew the base of retailers by sending Carlson the orders while he reinvented the product to address what brides really wanted, doing the work to reconfigure the presses himself.

In ten years Taylor had transformed Carlson from a small local print shop into a growing, regional presence. When Carlson was ready to retire, he sold to Taylor and two other employees—whom Taylor later bought out—for around $1 million, which Carlson agreed to let Taylor pay in installments over ten years. Taylor's strategy for growing the business and paying off the money he owed Carlson? Use invitations as the hook, and then advertise all of the other wedding accessories.

"Napkins were something we made a lot of money on," Taylor explained. "We sold the wedding invitations, and once we sell the wedding invitations the bride is getting all emotional about it and she wants the pretty things that accessorize. For napkins, I took an old press and took the heating coils from an old oven and I had a tube to turn it on and off out of a TV, and I got a celluloid tube off another machine, and with these changes the press made napkins. I earned half a million bucks a year. No one else could do it in the U.S. The old way, you had to handle the napkins once and then handle them again, but I built the machine to handle them just once and I could raise the price because it was such a unique product. It's like selling farm equipment. The dealer wants to sell the combine, but it is going to make $1 million on the parts." Taylor built and grew the business around the customer's needs, not around a narrower conception of what his company "did."

A BIAS TOWARD ACTION

Throughout the chapter we have focused on the tools and routes that billionaires take to come up with an idea—that combination of empathetic insight and practical imagination—that snowballs into a blockbuster hit. We emphasize the capacity with which our subjects balance the ability to understand what customers are going to embrace with the ability to imagine a new business that has broad, practical application.

We all know people who have ideas but do nothing to act on them, whether out of doubt or fear. When something is new and different, it's more easily ridiculed and dismissed, or approached using the wrong model. For every self-made billionaire, there are likely many more who observed a structural shift and had an idea of how to capitalize on that shift, but they either never tried or failed in the process.

"There's a lot of people that might have seen a similar paradigm shift," Lurie admitted to us when we asked what gave him the push to act on his vision of the merger of entertainment and sports. "But you need to—either through your own self-confidence or something else going on—you do need to complete that acquisition, otherwise you can just constantly ruminate about it. You know people that do that. They say, 'Oh, I could have done that, I could have done that, I could have done that.' So I don't know. I guess probably my obsession with the sport helped me make sure it was not just ruminating."

HOW CORPORATIONS CAN ENCOURAGE EMPATHY AND IMAGINATION

The ideas that Producers like Joe Mansueto, Jeff Lurie, Chip Wilson, Glen Taylor, Sara Blakely, Eli Broad, Dietrich Mateschitz, and dozens of others imagine and then pursue arrive through a powerful blend of empathy and imagination cultivated through years of immersion in a specific subject, curiosity, and, ultimately, courage. Good ideas are incredibly rare. Those that have that magic combination of empathy and imagination are even rarer. To increase your odds of having someone in-house discover one, make sure everyone is empowered to practice Empathetic Imagination. Businesses need as many people as possible looking for opportunities and coming up with ideas to capitalize on present and future trends. The trick is having a system and a culture that encourage people to surface ideas, with the understanding that the best among them will be supported and given the resources to go to market. We've provided some ideas for managers and corporate leaders below.

Cultivate Empathy

Start by cultivating empathy. Create opportunities for employees at all levels to understand firsthand what it is like to be a customer of your business. One way that vehicle manufacturers like Toyota and Harley-Davidson do this is by requiring employees to buy their vehicles using the same dealer network the customer uses. Other companies manufacture these experiences by having employees in different departments shadow sales calls or visit retail outlets to watch their products get sold. Others create pseudo–*Undercover Boss* scenarios and have employees pose as customers.[16]

These approaches and others give employees a new perspective on where the company excels and where it falls short. They can even reveal hidden opportunities or misconceptions about why the customer turns to you in the first place. It is in these exposures that purple oceans may reside. At the very least, these experiences can help uncover smaller customer irritations or even corporate attitudes that can and should be fixed. Such incremental improvement can clear away distractions that cloud up your day-to-day work, making bigger opportunities easier to spot.

Allow Employees to Own Their Ideas

To make empathy even more powerful, make sure employees have the ability and authority to act on what they see. Encourage people at all levels to look for and implement ways they can do their jobs better, be more productive, or deliver more value to the customer. These ideas may come from direct interaction with the customer; they may also come from experiences within the organization. Most ideas will be small, but they can empower people to embrace changes that redirect the business and make people at all levels feel that their contributions mean something, a seemingly minute action that can embolden people to present even more radical ideas.

Students of the "Lean" approach to change management will rightly see our encouragement for Lean-supported modes of thinking in these recommendations. Continuous improvement, one of the central tenets of the Toyota Production System from which Lean is derived, instills an organizational belief that processes and approaches can always get better, and that the people employed to do the work are in the best position to see opportunities in their zone of influence and act on them. In the realm of Empathetic Imagination, continuous improvement creates an environment in which small ideas have the potential to snowball into big ones, with the added benefit that it helps reveal the emergent Producers in your midst and gives them the opportunity to implement ideas.

Curiosity Breeds Big Ideas

Beyond empathy, embrace curiosity. Create rational opportunities for employees at all levels to learn about other areas of the business, other projects, or even other fields that are not immediately connected to their current area of focus.

The ultimate goal of practicing empathy, enabling incremental improvement, and encouraging curiosity is to Think Big—and sometimes to Act Big. Elevate conversations on big issues whether they are market trends, competitive threats, changes to the strategic landscape, or cultural challenges inside the organization. Address the real issues the business is facing in an open proactive approach that challenges everyone to imagine new solutions and connect the dots.

One example of a big issue that is top of mind in business environments today is data security, made evident by the high-profile breach suffered by Target in the 2013 Christmas shopping season. The credit card data of seventy million Target customers was reportedly hacked from the retailer's point-of-sale systems. This is clearly a big issue for Target and other retailers struggling to protect their reputations, but it is most often addressed by looking at the best practices of best-in-class retailers or financial companies to understand how they prevent security breaches. Natural Producers would look at the problem at a higher level, namely, how does the structure of the global credit card system compromise security and is there a global change that could improve it? In the same way that Walmart is influencing the environmental footprint of its global supply chain, could Target change the security footprint of retail payments? In this way, companies shift their organizational focus from day-to-day minutiae to the larger purpose of what the organization is about and what foundational solutions it can offer.

Questions at this level of scale are rarely posed at all, much less at all levels in corporate environments—another example of the ways that many large businesses constrain the collective imaginations of their employees. Thinking small is both safer for the careers of Producers who want to move up and, sadly, encouraged by the corporate

tendency to fund only those ideas a company can put in place immediately and count on for a short- to medium-term return.

One way to encourage employees to untether their imaginations is
to make clear your intention to stop navigating solely by the idea of core
competencies. Blockbuster ideas often leverage a Producer's knowledge
of an existing market, but they often attack that market through an entirely new mode. New modes require new competencies, or "value migration" as the theorist Adrian Slywotzky posits.[17] Producers can lead
the charge, but they need to be made to feel that they can have big ideas
that fall outside the company's core focus and that those ideas will be
taken seriously.

Companies that have already identified nascent Producers in their
midst by cultivating empathy, allowing employees to own their own
ideas, and giving opportunities for people to be curious can go to the
next level of signaling their willingness to embrace the new by creating
opportunities for experimentation. Newly identified, nascent Producers should be given opportunities to test a big idea—sometimes their
own—with actual customers. Only through real engagement in the
market can the Producer begin to hone, test, and revise to prepare the
idea for full-scale execution. Experimenting not only allows the business to test ideas and Producers but also sends a message to others
within the organization. When up-and-coming Producers see others
getting a chance to come up with and act upon big ideas, even put
something new out into the market, they will be better able to see how
their own potential can develop inside the firm and start to act on it.

Integrate Thinking and Doing

Do not isolate employees with big ideas (your thinkers) from the
workings—the doing—of the business. Especially when it applies to
coming up with new ideas and bringing them to market, you need to
bring together your creative resources—product developers, designers,

strategists, marketers—and your operational resources—your manufacturing and finance and supply chain—within cross-functional teams.

Most businesses, insofar as they have any imaginative talent at all, structure their organizations to isolate those whose primary role is to imagine from those whose primary role is to make decisions and take actions. Businesses separate these skills as a way to encourage innovation and dampen conflict, but the effect more often is to dampen the organization's capacity to mainstream innovation. Those with judgment have all the power; those with imagination operate in silos.

Our research has convinced us that one of the dominant Producer qualities is their integration of raw imagination with the judgment necessary to hone or manipulate a spark of empathetic insight to prepare it for market. The potential to come up with a blockbuster is that much greater exactly because the billionaire does not separate his ability to see what might be from his ability to assimilate and integrate it into what already exists. Corporate leaders, take note: don't separate thinking and doing. Instead, give integrated jobs to your emergent Producers that require them to both exhibit empathy and imagination, and have the freedom to make decisions about the best way to bring their ideas to market. That larger theme of execution is the subject of Chapter 4.

The last piece is to make clear how important the practice of empathy and imagination is to the business and to individual growth paths. Incorporate the practice of empathy and imagination into your evaluation system—for everyone. You aren't necessarily looking for output (you don't want to encourage people to shout out ideas just to be able to check off a box). Instead, you are creating ways for your managers to make room for imagination in their organizations, and to emphasize the importance of quality trend spotting, identifying problems, and creating useful solutions.

3

PATIENT URGENCY:
How Billionaires Thrive Despite
the Uncertainty of Time

They always say time changes things, but you actually
have to change them yourself.
—ANDY WARHOL

roupon founder Eric Lefkofsky has a clear vision of the imaginative ideas he wants to support now and a decade from now. "Ideas
that are local, social, and mobile in orientation are going to do well in
the next ten years," he told us in December 2012 when we met at his
office in Chicago. That's the idea behind Groupon, which Lefkofsky
launched in 2008, and the operating philosophy of Lightbank, the
venture capital firm he runs with his business partner Brad Keywell.
"Our long-term theme is that biotech and life sciences are eventually
going to be as exciting as the Internet has been in the past decade, but
we aren't in that space yet."[1]

Waiting for the right time to get into markets like biotech and life
sciences requires patience. For those markets he keeps up on the

research and pays attention, from a distance, to the small companies doing interesting things. Watch him work on the areas that he sees as big *now,* however, and Lefkofsky exudes urgency. Lefkofsky pressures management teams of his portfolio companies to get products into the hands of customers as quickly as possible so they can learn through direct experience.

"We do everything quickly," Lefkofsky says of the process he uses when one of his portfolio companies needs to bring product to the market. "When you are an entrepreneur building a tech company you are likely making mistakes based on lack of experience and you are likely running out of money. You don't have that long of a fuse. So we work hard at compressing cycles and preparing to pivot. Most of that is being unwilling to tolerate the longer timeline. It is just saying we don't have a month, we need it done in two weeks."

Consistent with that view, Lefkofsky does not hesitate to pull the plug when the market sends the message that an idea does not resonate. He said, "We have been more successful than most, not because of our investing capability, but because we are good at getting in there and saying we are setting some objective criteria, and if we don't meet these milestones we have to pivot and go in a different direction. And it is really hard because when you miss the milestone no one wants to pivot. Everyone is in denial believing you are going to get the next version out and it will all be better. It's like admitting you're an alcoholic—the signs are there and 99.9 percent of the time the signs are not wrong."

THE DUALITY OF TIME

Lefkofsky's attitudes toward time may seem contradictory. He has a long-term vision of the kinds of businesses he wants to be involved with, but an intense focus on the short-term actions necessary to test the companies whose time is now. Put another way, he exhibits patience with the ideas he believes are right but for which the market is not yet ready. Then, when the market is ripe, he acts urgently to get the product into the hands of customers and looks for immediate feedback. Producers successfully marry patience and urgency, creating a dual perspective on time.

In the previous chapter on Empathetic Imagination, we talked about how Producers see and emphasize major trends, and how they develop blockbuster ideas to capitalize on the opportunities those trends reveal. From Jeffrey Lurie's vision of a structural shift that would merge sports and entertainment, to Joe Mansueto's view of mutual funds as an emerging mainstream product, to Lefkofsky's idea of a present and near future in which business models leverage local, social, and mobile, these Producers are driven first by an idea with the potential to bring huge value at enormous scale—they don't waste their time on small ideas. But once they've hit on a compelling idea or market space, Producers are sensitive to issues of time. If it's too soon, the idea may die for lack of demand; too late and another player may have already redefined the market.

Our research uncovered no consistent evidence that Producers are better prognosticators than other people—they cannot predict the exact right time to make an investment or bring a product to market. The difference is that Producers are willing to operate simultaneously at multiple speeds and time frames. Producers accept that timing is not under their control, and with that acceptance they come to the market aware— and accommodating of the fact—that time is not static but elastic. The fixed nature of the quarter is irrelevant. Time can speed up or slow down at will, and so Producers must work at fast, slow, and super-slow speeds all at the same time, and switch quickly between these modes depending on the context: urgency around actions that are needed to set the stage for realizing an opportunity; patience when they have to wait.

An important nuance in their dual-time mind-set is that duration does not determine mode. We often think of patience as the right mind-set when the wait is long; urgency when we need to produce an outcome under a strict deadline. But these distinctions are irrelevant to Producers. They may act with constant urgency over years, even decades; they may need to be patient for just a few weeks or months. The important distinction is their flexibility and balanced tacking between the two, not the time frames in which they apply them.

TIMING, FAST AND SLOW

Eric Lefkofsky's early career offers a look into how an emergent Producer learns hard lessons about time over many years. More than a decade before Lightbank and Groupon, Lefkofsky and Keywell were the proprietors of BrandOn, a brick-and-mortar retailer that specialized in licensed apparel. Focused on children's clothing, they sold T-shirts and onesies with football team logos and other branded images. The company was in its fifth year and struggling just as the Internet went mainstream, so Lefkofsky and Keywell started to examine whether they could shift platforms to take advantage of the technology trends.

"We realized that we had become very good at decorating stuff in small lot sizes," Lefkofsky told us about their thinking at the time. "We were very good at making twelve or twenty-four or six of something instead of making ten thousand. And we thought small companies on the Internet, all of a sudden, can access and afford promotional products in ways that they probably couldn't historically. So, if you want to buy twelve golf balls for your golf outing or twenty-four hats for a small company, you can buy them."

Lefkofsky and Keywell decided to switch their focus to pursue the idea of creating branded swag for small businesses, but within less than a year the Internet bubble burst, taking their new Web-based enterprise down with it. "The entrance to market was way ahead of its time," Lefkofsky said. "That business, maybe, would just start to get some traction today. But at the time it was way too early."

This early experience helps explain the origins of Lefkofsky's long-term, patient commitment to technology-based business models that leverage the Internet and mobile systems. It also explains how Lefkofsky developed the perspective he uses to evaluate and guide companies in the Lightbank portfolio—he knows from experience that an idea before its time will either wither and die in the market, or require a lot of capital and a long leash.

The Groupon idea was, for a long time, one of these premature concepts. "People tried a very similar business model ten years before," Lefkofsky said. "Mercado was one and it just didn't take off. The timing to market is very tricky, but once you have all the different ingredients that are necessary, some of these businesses can really catch fire. In the case of Groupon, we needed a social layer to be built that didn't exist in the late nineties when there was no Facebook, no Twitter, no word of mouth."

Once that social layer was created, the time for Groupon arrived and the company entered the urgent phase, experiencing explosive growth leading up to its initial public offering. Now the firm is in a mixed state, urgently focused on improving its operations and preventing imitators from catching up, while trying to exercise the patience that so often is needed after a company reaches significant scale.

LESSONS IN TIMING

Eric Lefkofsky is not the only billionaire who has experience with getting the timing wrong. Sunil Mittal, the billionaire founder of Bharti

Enterprises, is another with firsthand experience with catastrophic timing.

Mittal started his first business in 1976 selling bicycles and bicycle parts in Ludhiana, Punjab, where, he said, "Everyone is an entrepreneur of some kind."[2] Mittal soon saw that his bicycle business had a limit to how big it could get, so he moved to Mumbai (Bombay at the time) and switched to selling a variety of imported products—he saw the development of India, a growing middle class, and a demand for products that were available in other countries but scarce in India. Soon he was importing portable generators through a partnership with Suzuki, and starting to make some real money, right up until 1983 when the Indian government issued a ban on imported generators. From one day to the next, Mittal was out of business.

Arguably he got into imported generators at exactly the *wrong* time. But from the rubble of his collapsed business he preserved the core concept of importing established products for which there was low supply and high demand in India. He had existing relationships with a number of foreign businesses, and a proven track record as a reliable partner. Those connections made it easier for Mittal to persuade large manufacturers to partner with him to bring their products to India, whose economy was otherwise closed to foreign competitors until the 1991 economic reforms.

With those relationships as his focus, Mittal took some time after his generator business collapsed to travel to Japan, Korea, and Taiwan to identify other products he might be able to import and sell. His experience of losing a business at the hands of a regulatory change was top of mind, and likely informed the product he ultimately chose—touch-tone phones and, later, cellular devices, which he imported on behalf of major manufacturers and sold across the Indian subcontinent (India didn't have any native manufacturers of those products at the time). Establishing his business in phones allowed him to urgently learn about the telecommunications market over many years of first importing and later manufacturing telecommunications hardware. By the 1990s, Mittal was in a position to establish Airtel and urgently bought one of the telecommunications licenses that the Indian government was issuing as part of the process of privatizing more of its industries. Today, Airtel is one of the largest telecommunications companies in India, a company made possible by good timing learned from a bad experience.

Tadashi Yanai, the billionaire CEO of Fast Retailing Co., owner of the Uniqlo brand of mass-market clothing stores, was more fortunate than Mittal with the timing of his first business. When Yanai was coming of age in the 1980s, his father owned a group of stores that made formal men's suits, a typical clothing business in Japan at the time. In fact, Japan's penchant for formality was reflected in an underpopulated clothing industry made up of small-scale retailers that produced formal clothing, each company focusing on either men or women. As Yanai explains it, "There weren't many stores selling casual clothes back then. Clothing stores sold suits, like the one you're wearing, or formal wear. Casual clothes meant cheap clothing for young people."[3]

Yanai initially had no intention of getting into his father's business, but ultimately conceded when he found himself postcollege with no job and no real desire to do anything else. He nonetheless knew he didn't just want to do what his father had done. Yanai had already traveled a bit at that point in his life and he had seen what clothing retail looked like in other countries. He'd seen the low prices of "Made in China" retail items in Hong Kong; he'd seen the ubiquitous popularity of The Gap in the United States, and of Marks & Spencer in Great Britain, brands that sold classic staples at affordable prices. Japan didn't have any similar brands. There was a gap in the market, which Yanai had the Empathetic Imagination to see, and then acted with urgency to fill. In 1984, he launched his first Uniqlo store in Hiroshima to sell high-quality casual classics at affordable prices.

"What we did was change that image of casual clothing into practical and comfortable clothing. We discovered and created a completely new market."[4] In just seven years, Uniqlo was on its way to becoming Japan's largest casual clothing retailer, with thirty-three stores opened in 1990 alone.

Yanai without a doubt had excellent timing. He saw a gap in the Japanese market, and he had the empathetic insight that young Japanese men and women of his generation would want alternatives to their parents' clothing. Yanai saw a purple ocean where timing was of the essence, and he set out to exploit it, growing Uniqlo with Patient Urgency over a period of decades until it became the largest clothing retailer in Japan. More recently, Uniqlo has been expanding internationally, with stores in major urban centers in China, the United States, and Europe.

Good Timing Comes with Preparation

Producers whose blockbuster ideas depend upon an emergent or future trend do not innately know when the time is right. All the Producers we spoke with were entirely forthright on that point—they didn't know *when* their vision was going to become a reality. But they didn't just dive in and hope for the best either. Their faith in the idea itself made them sure that they needed to be ready when the time came, and that readiness required preparation, in a number of forms, from learning about the market to early investments and market positions.

"It wasn't that I was aware of the timing of it," Jeffrey Lurie, the Philadelphia Eagles owner, said of his vision of the coming convergence of sports and entertainment. "It wasn't like I knew two years after I bought the team there was going to be a big escalation in value. It was that I thought it was going to happen."

Similarly, Joe Mansueto told us, "I could not have seen thirty years ago what Morningstar looks like today, and even today I can't see thirty years from now. I can see a year or two ahead. I have some idea of things that we should consider longer-term. But it's very much one foot ahead of the other. It's like running a marathon—you don't think 'I've got twenty two miles to go.' But rather, 'I'm at mile two, and I want to get to mile three.' It's that kind of mind-set. But I always thought if we compound at a good growth rate, we'd be big soon enough. I always thought we had a good future. But I couldn't articulate exactly what that would look like in five, ten, or fifteen years. I knew we were doing things that were valuable to people. We'll continue to stay focused and build on that philosophy."

Operating in a world of inevitable uncertainty requires not only an ability to balance patience and urgency, but a sense of equanimity about when you need which the most. Instant, explosive, and exclusively upward growth is not what the majority of self-made billionaires experience. We spent a lot of time mapping the career trajectory of Producers, an exercise that clearly revealed that the most common path was a long progression of steady growth that includes significant setbacks and even business failures, as well as steep gains and accomplishments. Many billionaires are serial entrepreneurs, hitting the mother lode not on their first but on their second, third, or fourth try.

Building value over an extended period of time when the outcomes are not guaranteed requires a willingness to be ready, all the time, for the opportunities yet to come. As billionaires pursue their blockbuster ideas, they show a great deal of patience for how, and how fast, they grow. But exhibiting patience does not mean they are sitting back and letting things happen on their own time. In fact, they are acting all the time—they are making deals, testing ideas in the market, and looking for improvements and adjustments. The time frames are measured in years, even decades, during which they are striving and acting with urgency in pursuit of value that may take years to unveil.

Building a Marathon Mind-Set

For Steve Case, the wait lasted ten years. Twenty, actually, if you consider that he started thinking about the kind of business he wanted to be a part of as a senior at Williams College.[5]

"It was the late seventies and I was trying to think about what I was going to do," Case told us in the Washington, D.C., offices of his venture capital firm, Revolution. "I just felt like I would be most interested in something that was emerging and be part of a revolution as opposed to a more traditional company that was just managing. I wanted to be part of creating something new," he said.

At that time Case read *The Third Wave* by Alvin and Heidi Toffler, futurists who predicted the development and popularity of an Internet-like connected network. Case said, "I was captivated by the idea that someday people would access each other and get information and be able to buy products through this new interactive technology. At the time the focus was more on how TV would become more interactive because PCs hadn't really emerged. I just remember reading that and saying, 'I just know this is going to happen. It's such an obvious idea.' That really kind of became the guiding light in terms of my life."

There were no companies Case could find creating consumer networks at that time, so he decided to wait and use his time learning the basics of business, first at Procter & Gamble and, later, in the Pizza Hut division of PepsiCo. While working for these iconic firms he had the explicit goal, as he tells it, of gaining key business skills so he would be ready when the opportunity he was waiting for arrived.

The opportunity came in 1984, when Case's brother, a venture capitalist, introduced him to the lead executives of a D.C.-based start-up called Control Video, which was making an early-stage interactive gaming network for Atari users. "People didn't have PCs at the time but they did have Atari game machines," Case said. "So this company created a product for the game machine, and although that was a struggle and ultimately it was unsuccessful, it was a way for me to get into the start-up world. And some of the people I met there did end up joining me and starting AOL in 1985, a couple of years later."

The idea for AOL as a network service provider was stable from the beginning, but there was a lot of foundational work that needed to be done in order to create a mainstream communications network capable of handling traffic from a mass market. Case and AOL had to negotiate and partner with device manufacturers, network service providers, and motivate staff to create the systems that would be needed for AOL to deliver at scale. The company had to advocate for the integration of network capability into PCs, ensure network service, and build user-friendly software.

Case said, "For the better part of a decade after we started AOL it was a struggle. I used to say AOL was an overnight success ten years in the making. By the mid-to-late nineties, when the Internet came into focus, new people were joining AOL in large numbers, and the brand was on the cover of a magazine, it looked like AOL just kind of popped out of nowhere and it was an instant success. But we'd been at it for nearly a decade trying to fine-tune and get the computers to include a communications modem installed instead of viewing it as a peripheral, and get the network costs down so we could charge less for our service, and get the software better so it was friendly or more engaging for a mainstream market, and get the content more interesting. There were a lot of building blocks."

As Case makes clear, patient time spent waiting for an idea to mature is not the same as idle time. Building a business with huge growth potential requires not only a marathon mind-set, as Joe Mansueto put it, but also marathon action—Producers are moving all the time.

Urgent Self-Preparation

Case's early, postcollege years spent learning about business and marketing gels with what we discussed in the previous chapter about Empathetic Imagination: namely, that most Producers start their billion-dollar businesses after amassing extensive experience in the industries or areas where they ultimately create breakthrough value. Even those who earn billionaire status at a relatively young age seem to have that hard-fought expertise. Many develop it by using "wait time"— those months or years after they have an empathetic insight but before the market is ready—to prep themselves for coming opportunity.

Like Steve Case, Joe Mansueto was in his early twenties when he first had the idea that would become Morningstar. But also like Case, Mansueto knew he did not yet know enough about the world of business—in his case, investing and the market for investment research—to build a business in that space. And mutual funds were only just starting to grow as a mainstream investment. Mansueto had wait time, and he used it by spending a few years in personal education before he launched Morningstar.

With a sense of urgency, he took a crash course in mutual funds and personal investing. He took a job first with the Chicago venture capital firm Golder Thoma, where he stayed but four months, and then with a boutique money management firm called Harris Associates, which managed to hold on to him for slightly more than a year. In both places he thrived, receiving high marks from his superiors. Still, less than two years after he first had the idea, a more experienced, knowledgeable, and established Mansueto left Harris Associates to launch Morningstar.

One of his first actions was to put an advertisement in *Barron's* announcing a $130 subscription to his quarterly *Mutual Fund Sourcebook,* the first edition of which he wrote sitting at the kitchen table of his one-bedroom apartment. That first ad generated six hundred orders—$78,000 worth of revenue—and he began his upward climb to becoming a billionaire.

ACTING URGENTLY ON AN INSTINCT

Like Steve Case, Alex Spanos, a billionaire real estate developer, also had to wait for the time to be right before capitalizing on his idea, but that is where the similarities between the two end. Case worked in a communications start-up, where he then had to wait as the market matured over the better part of a decade. Spanos, by contrast, began his entrepreneurial career thrust into a market in which demand already far outstripped existing supply. When he set up his first independent venture, he had to act fast, with positive results and clear signals of success accruing almost immediately—much more quickly than the decade Case spent building the systems and demand for AOL.[6] Viewed together, these stories illustrate the various ways in which patience and urgency operate for any individual Producer, and independently from the time frames involved.

Spanos was born in the 1920s to Greek immigrants. He spent most of his twenties working as a baker in his father's small bakery in Stockton, California. According to Spanos, his dad was dictatorial and stingy with pay, and eventually the younger Spanos—driven by the need for more financial stability for himself and his growing family—went out on his own. Spanos was twenty-seven and had no savings, but he was an experienced baker and he'd been running his father's business for many years, in that role becoming a known figure within the Stockton small-business community. He was also observant—as he drove to work in the early hours of the morning each day he saw the seasonal workers buying their meals for the day from food stands set up near the fields of the local San Joaquin Valley farmers.

As a first step, Spanos got a loan from the bank, bought supplies, and started making sandwiches. Every day he prepared enough for hundreds of workers, and within weeks he was earning more than when he had worked for his dad. But he was ambitious, so when the farm owner approached him one day asking if he knew where to find more workers, Spanos worked with urgency. It was high picking season and the crop was almost ripe—all the farmers in the area needed more workers to harvest the produce before it rotted in the fields. Spanos got on a bus the next morning and traveled to Mexicali, where workers came to get hired by farm agents. While there, Spanos spoke with an agent recruiting not only for the same farmer who had approached Spanos, but also for other farmers in the San Joaquin Valley. The agent told him that the problem wasn't only recruiting people but finding temporary shelter while they were in town. Spanos said he could take care of it—if the agent got the workers, Spanos would find them someplace to stay.

At the time, that was all bravado. Spanos later admitted he had no idea how to house hundreds, let alone thousands, of workers, and his experience with catering was limited to sandwich making.[7] But he didn't hesitate to make a fast decision, and he made good on it. He knew a lot about Stockton, and he knew that the local fairgrounds had a large hangar-type building that sat empty most of the year. After another quick bank loan and a set of negotiations, he was able to set up hundreds of cots in the hangar. Outside, he built a cooking tent where he prepared classic rice, beans, tortillas, and other recipes hewing to the tastes and traditions of the Mexicans he served. He also scheduled a bus service to bring workers to the fields and then back again. In that first season, he netted $60,000 in 1951 dollars mere months after setting out on his own—that is equivalent to more than half a million dollars in buying power today. Within four years in a business notable for its grueling work schedule and around-the-clock hours, Spanos was a millionaire and preparing to set out on his next phase of growth as a real estate developer, a path which would, with patience and care, turn him into the largest builder of apartment housing in the United States.

TIME AND IMAGINATION

All businesses are under pressure to deliver results in specific time intervals. Billionaires don't necessarily make exceptions, as Eric Lefkofsky's "milestones" attest. But there is a distinction between the ways in which Producers act with urgency, and the typical corporate environment of overextending talent. For most institutions there are simply too many tasks to complete in too little time, and that overextension can have a detrimental effect.

People at all levels of business justify overwork by saying it makes us more efficient, or that time pressure spurs creativity, but the reality is more insidious. In fact, time pressure can suppress the imagination necessary to come up with blockbuster ideas.

There are physiological mechanisms at work when people are engaging in imaginative thought processes. Rex Jung, a neuropsychologist from the University of New Mexico, posits that creative people are able to turn off the evaluative functions of their brains in order to allow themselves mental freedom to invent.[8] He calls this process *transient hypofrontality,* which is just a technical way of saying that the analytical mechanisms of the brain take a break for a while to let imagination run free.

Where does time come in? Jung argues that hugely imaginative people—think pure Producers—engage in transient hypofrontality automatically, *but anyone can create the environment* that allows them to shut down their analytical capabilities and just allow ideas to wander and associations to take place. In order to achieve this state, however, the aspiring creative needs *time*. He or she needs to be in an environment where mind wandering can happen.

A number of innovation-oriented companies have made headlines for giving employees permission to take a certain percentage of their time to explore new ideas, but it is definitely a minority practice. Even when such a policy is in place, there is often pressure for measurable results to emerge from the "free time." For most professionals there is such a dramatic mismatch between what they are expected to produce and the amount of time they are given to produce it in that the opportunities to induce *transient hypofrontality* are virtually nonexistent. Such time pressure essentially guarantees that professionals won't have the mental space to come up with blockbuster ideas.

If this connection seems abstract, consider the results from a study on time and creativity conducted by a group of researchers at Harvard Business School.[9] The research team enlisted seven companies and 177 employees in a study to assess whether workers under time pressure are able to produce work of high creative value. The researchers collected daily questionnaires from the workers asking them to assess whether they were under pressure that day, how much they got done, and how creative the output was. They also collected data from the company on daily task assignments and deadlines to confirm that the workers' feelings of being under time pressure reflected real time pressure based on more objective information (they did), and they collected assessments from managers on the level of creativity exhibited by the participating employees.

The results showed an inverse relationship between time pressure and creative output. Employees often got more done on high-pressure days—meaning that they were more efficient—but the level of creativity in their output was low. This finding alone is important to our understanding of the relationship between time and business creativity. But even more compelling was the fact that the low creative output *persisted*. One day of high time pressure resulted in lower creative output for *days* after.

Self-made Billionaire Time Management

Understanding the relationship between time and creativity gave us insight into a tendency that we observed firsthand in the billionaires we met. That habit could be best described as being *present*.

It was one of the first things we noticed about Joe Mansueto, for example. When we walked into Morningstar's office on the day of our meeting, he was sitting at a table in a conference room with his hands crossed over each other, *waiting for us*. "Yes," he said, "I am ready for you." We expected that our time with him would be interrupted by other obligations, questions, or commitments, but that wasn't the case, neither with him, nor with Glen Taylor, Chip Wilson, Jeff Lurie, Steve Case, T. Boone Pickens, or the Spanos children. When we were with Mansueto, it seemed as if our interview was the only commitment he had. His phone didn't ring. No one entered the room in the middle of the conversation to give him a message. He was completely present.

This trait is almost universal among the billionaires we interviewed. They were focused, attentive, and entirely present as we spoke. Steve Case even thanked *us* for taking the time to talk with him about the research we were doing and the ideas we wanted to explore. We call attention to this trait because it is so different from our daily interactions with the executives we work with—our colleagues, our clients, even ourselves. We all seem to be doing three things at once *in addition to* having a conversation with someone. Not so with the billionaires. They appear far less busy than most executives, and we suspect that isn't an accident of seniority. They intentionally guard their time, doing away with extras, distractions, and nonessential activities so that they are able to support their most vital work.

By guarding their time preciously billionaires are able to constantly cultivate and grow their innate curiosity. It gives them the time to read or converse widely on the subjects that let them make remote connections.

We cannot say that such strict time management *causes* success, but the evidence is strong in support of the idea that disciplined— even ritualistic—practices open up the mental space to observe long-term trends and develop a compelling and real vision around them.

A Producer's ability to be present in the "now" has implications for the evolution and success of her business. Just as Producers limit the number of things they are involved in to allow for enough attention and energy to focus on growing the blockbuster, they also have the ability to know exactly where they are in their business. They don't go off track planning for the next stage before they have capitalized on the present. They don't spend too much time sizing and resizing the market before they have a concept and prototype they can show to people.

As an example, if you think about the evolution of Alex Spanos's business, his actions were progressive and he focused exactly on where he was at any given time. When the opportunity lay in making sandwiches for the farmworkers, he focused on building his capacity to make sandwiches. When the opportunity lay in feeding and providing housing for thousands of migrants, he focused on building the capacity and infrastructure to feed and house thousands. He did not start planning to serve five thousand workers before he had served a thousand. All those migrant workers were customers using the service and offering feedback.

We refer to the ability Producers have to focus on the challenge at hand as "stage focus." We dedicate Chapter 4 to discussing Inventive Execution, of which stage focus is an integral part. As this quality relates to time, the Producers' ability to keep the vision of long-term scale in the back of their minds while concentrating their current energies on urgent execution for today is critical to their success. Stage focus allows them to make their blockbuster idea real in the market and meet necessary targets before moving to the next stage of growth and execution.

HOW EXECUTIVES CAN APPLY THE LESSONS OF PATIENT URGENCY

Businesses have understood time's integral role in the success or failure of commerce since the early days of trade. As far back as 1736, when the British inventor John Harrison conducted the first sea test of the marine chronometer, a device that used time to accurately estimate a ship's latitude and longitude at sea, businesses were dealing with the challenge posed by the uncertainty of time. Before Harrison's invention, sea captains could only identify *latitude* by measuring the angle of the sun at noon, when it reached its apex, but without an accurate timepiece they had no way to measure longitude, and so quite literally had no idea where in the world they were at any given moment. Armed with a chronometer, sea captains could now navigate with more accuracy, avoid dangerous routes, and effectively decrease the length of their journeys. Harrison's invention changed the business of seafaring—and set the British on a path to extreme value creation in trade.

Fast-forward nearly two hundred years and Frederick Winslow Taylor, the father of scientific management, was using time and motion studies to develop ideas to help businesses improve their productivity.

Time measurement also made possible the digital computer, which samples itself billions of times a second and records its data through binary impulses—on or off—within a defined window of time.

We offer these examples because they show how business innovators of the past have leveraged time as a tool, a source of invention or advantage, or at least as a dynamic factor in their ideation. As a group, self-made billionaires subscribe to this time-value school of competitive advantage. They talk about time in dramatically different ways from the typical corporate executive, for whom time is often a limiting factor or a constraint imposed upon them by the board, C-suite executives, the stock market, or simply years of corporate training.

Readers may also think that the Producers experience with time is less instructive because billionaires have so much control over how their businesses are run. And while we agree that billionaires have a lot of control at the beginning, once their businesses reach scale—and especially those that go public—they experience the same fixed-time-frame mentality that hampers the pursuit of value in so many companies. Yet these Producers still don't let time define them or their ideas.

Joe Mansueto spoke directly about this issue in the context of cultivating an entrepreneurial mind-set within a mature organization. He said, "It gets more challenging as we get bigger because we understandably have policies and processes around doing things. It's important to have the necessary reviews in place, but you want to be sure it doesn't prevent you from being nimble."

Corporations establish these processes to help keep bad ideas out of the market. But Mansueto believes they need balance. "We try not to let the process define us," he said. "The process is not the product. We focus on execution to get things done. You have to have some process, but you can't get so wrapped up in it that you move too slowly. Individually all those processes sound logical but cumulatively they could be the death knell for great products."

Mansueto's attitude illustrates the ways that Producers recognize time issues, but do not let time attitudes suppress or trump ideas. At the core of the Producers' ability to maintain a dual perspective on time is a belief in and passion for the idea they are pursuing. Across our study, we saw Producers consistently dedicate their time only to ideas that had the potential to build massive value. Not all of these ventures were successful, but the vision and intent was to build something real at scale. With an idea in hand, Producers then manifest a balance of utmost urgency with extreme patience. They'll wait for the time to be right, but they will prepare relentlessly so that they are ready to jump on the opportunity when it arrives.

How can established corporations build more of this Patient Urgency into their businesses?

Move Beyond the Quarter

Corporations first must relax the way they think about the time frames within which they pursue new opportunities. Reconsider any in-house expectations about when you expect return on an investment. Do you eschew new initiatives if they take longer than two years to produce a return? Three years? Five? Do you expect concrete results to register in quarterly intervals? The billionaire Producers, despite their universal interest in strong returns, made it clear that the ideas worth pursuing may also be worth waiting for. Producers engage in the pursuit, and they use the wait time to their advantage to develop expertise, knowledge, market positions, partnerships, and other necessary resources so that when the market is ready they are already there.

In contrast, traditional organizations, though used to waiting, are rarely skilled at *urgent* waiting—those quarters or years spent putting the skills and resources in place so the business is ready when the opportunity arrives, just as Steve Case urgently built AOL over ten years before the Internet exploded. More often than not, companies take a pass today and say they will get back to it later (and later is often too late).

Bottom line: organizations that consistently turn down opportunities because the time frames do not match their accustomed cycles are leaving value on the table. The institution implicitly sets criteria for the kinds of ideas it wants, which not only dictates what leaders choose to pursue but also signals to emergent Producers to constrain their Empathetic Imaginations. Producers who have good ideas with uncertain timing may either keep them under wraps or, if they're good enough, leave to pursue them outside the firm's walls.

There are a number of steps applicable at different levels to help businesses begin to relax this organizational rigidity about time.

Individual Time Management

At the most individual level, task individuals throughout the organization to reconsider their standard time scales. Ask your direct reports to reconsider what time frame is needed for a project to come to fruition. Is it shorter than you planned? Longer? Would it be shorter if the project participants weren't tasked with too many other responsibilities of lower priority? Don't accept predefined/benchmarked time frames when they don't make sense. Propose an alternative and work with Patient Urgency to prove how right you are about it.

Another step is to give those who show Producer potential special "think time" and consider making it truly open to whatever they are interested in pursuing. Steve Jobs was famous for the long walks he took, often with a colleague or a new business partner. Readers of Walter Isaacson's biography of the Apple founder may have read it as a mark of Jobs's eccentricity, but in light of what we have learned about time and the role it plays in stimulating the imagination, we wonder if those walks weren't Jobs's way of letting his synapses fire.[10]

Regardless, it's clear to us that the standard practice of rewarding our most promising talent by giving them *more* to do is wrong. If we want emergent Producers to have a chance to identify the next blockbuster, give them less and see what happens.

These two acts of challenging employees to consider the time frames of their work and giving them think time should make clear who in your team has the capacity for trend spotting. Narrow in on those people capable of seeing trends or activities that others overlook or view as inconsequential. Some of these trend spotters will even be able to see further out—two, even three years. Some of them may already be experts in a particular subject, or have displayed a long-term commitment to an area of expertise. These individuals are particularly valuable, given the overwhelming tendency of billionaire Producers to find and pursue new opportunities in fields where they already have extensive experience. And for those who see important trends and have a high-potential idea for how to capitalize on it, consider matching their think time with "explore time" earmarked for taking steps to design and execute the idea.

Producers will thrive when asked to match such "thinking" with "doing." It benefits the organization by bringing good ideas to the next level and it can help weed out Vision Performers from true Producers. Vision Performers will see future trends, and may even develop an idea to capitalize on them, but they will get mired in what needs to happen right away; Producers, in contrast, have the integrative ability to see past today's requirements to focus on what is needed for the future. Look for and cultivate those with savvy skills around the "politics of time." Eventually, the Producers who rise need to be able to stand up to investor pressure to speed up or abandon a program that is taking longer to produce returns than the investor wants. R&D in particular is vulnerable to the time-based chopping block and will need staunch defenders.

Timing in the Organization

There are a few changes to processes and procedures that can help loosen organizational rigidity around time. One seemingly simple step is to communicate corporate goals in multiple time frames. Just as Eric Lefkofsky has a future vision of opportunity in biotech and life sciences, and a current vision of mobile and social, so should your organization signal its goals for today and its goals for tomorrow. Identifying these goals and communicating them broadly gives the Empathetic Imaginations in your organization permission to consider today *and* tomorrow when they look for new opportunities.

For ideas that have already been given a green light, likewise consider the relative time the corporation spends on different stages compared with Producers. Producers worry a lot about the concept, but they don't spend time scrutinizing it through more discussion, thought, and analysis. As we highlighted in the chapter on Empathetic Imagination, Producers have a bias toward action, which shows itself in the propensity to make ideas real and operational so they can be tested with actual customers. When developing an idea, they move quickly from concept to prototype, which they then test with a small group of customers, and launch in a limited capacity. They work the concept by engaging with its real manifestation, not by wasting time worrying about the theoretical analysis. In this way Producers get their products or services into the hands of potential customers as quickly as possible, and then rework based on that real market experience.

Joe Mansueto, for example, didn't spend months talking to potential clients and testing his idea when launching Morningstar. He had such faith in the inherent value of what he was doing that he took out an ad, wrote the first publication, and got it into the hands of the investors. Changes came quickly, but they were based on direct engagement with the customer.

In contrast, the businesses we know and work with spend long months in concept and prototype, investing significant brainpower *internally* to estimate market size, conduct focus groups, analyze the in-house capacity and skill sets, and assess other in-house execution-based measures. By the time they get to launch, they have invested significant time and money on theoretical models. They've cut their own time windows short and created a much lower margin for error. They almost *have* to succeed right away or leave the market. This approach makes it harder than it needs to be to experiment or pivot.

Lastly, explore ways and means that your organization can be involved in business areas or trends that are not yet on your strategic horizon, but you think may be in the future. All of the above steps are aimed at identifying the Producers in your organization and giving them the space to produce far more value. But it remains that you won't be able to pursue every idea on the table, even some that are very good. Indeed, it is something of a business truism that corporations that work relentlessly in pursuit of between one and three strategic priorities do more and achieve more than those that try to pursue six or eight at one time. Maintaining Patient Urgency in areas that may become interesting to you in the future, but aren't yet, invites you to partner with organizations that are focused in that field, such as academic institutions or start-ups. Staying engaged in this way may allow you to save yourself a seat at that table without drawing resources away from your most urgent pursuits.

4

INVENTIVE EXECUTION:
How Producers Bring Blockbusters to Market

Don't worry about people stealing an idea. If it's original,
you will have to ram it down their throats.
—HOWARD AIKEN

When Michael Jaharis and his business partner Phillip Frost bought Miami-based Key Pharmaceuticals in 1972, they thought they were buying a healthy enterprise with some modest products, a strong foundation from which they could grow. But that hope vanished a few weeks later when Jaharis went to Washington, D.C., for a meeting at the FDA.[1]

"I sat in on a cardiovascular meeting alongside a group of the top cardio people, who were there to advise the FDA with respect to a new law that required drug companies to prove drug efficacy," Jaharis told us when we sat down with him in the New York offices of Vatera Healthcare Partners, a health-care venture capital firm he cofounded after selling KOS Pharmaceuticals to Abbott Laboratories.

One of Key Pharmaceuticals' main products at the time was a long-acting nitroglycerin pill whose sole market distinction was its purported ability to be long acting. "They said it doesn't work," Jaharis told us. "One of the experts, Dr. Philip Needleman, had conducted a series of lab experiments, and his studies showed that long-acting oral nitroglycerin just didn't work. So, at that point I knew I was in trouble. And, it was around the same time that we found out the previous managers of Key hadn't given me an accurate financial picture, so that instead of being profitable, the company had really lost $700,000 in the previous year with annual sales of $1.5 million. So we were in terrible shape starting off, to say the least."

Most executives would have responded by jettisoning the offending product or casting around for a new one. But Jaharis took a different tack—he redesigned the products he had. At that time, nitroglycerin was delivered exclusively in pill form. Those pills took a few minutes to make their way into the bloodstream and were used up quickly, even the supposedly long-acting ones. While at the same meeting in Washington, Jaharis had heard Dr. Needleman talk about a nitroglycerin topical application, which was deployed as an ointment on the skin and absorbed continuously throughout the day. Unlike the oral tablet, the ointment had the potential to be effective as long-acting nitroglycerin.

Jaharis also heard about the use of patches to deliver medication, and had a version developed for Key's topical nitroglycerin. (A similar approach would be used ten years later by Murray Jarvik, the inventor of the nicotine patch, as an aid in smoking cessation.) The resulting Nitro-Dur nitroglycerin patch became a flagship of the Key Pharmaceuticals portfolio, and set the company on a path of profitability that led to its 1986 acquisition for $836 million by Schering-Plough.

INVENTIVE EXECUTION BEGINS WITH DESIGN

The approach Jaharis used to turn a failing pharmaceutical firm into an $800 million business highlights the inventiveness that Producers use to execute their ideas. Through the practice of Empathetic Imagination, they home in on business ideas with large-scale potential, but creating blockbuster value requires not just ideas but also an inventive approach to making those ideas manifest in the market. These are separate skills: the ability to dream *and* act, imagine what is possible *and* design it in a way that captures the greatest value.

The steps Jaharis took to save Key Pharmaceuticals reveal how a true Producer will reinvent seemingly small, fixed, and immovable aspects of the business design to extract the most value. Producers can think small—in Jaharis's case by concentrating on how a medication is delivered—in order to capture something large—demand for a continuous-release nitroglycerin.

We use the verb "design" in this context to describe the solutions to the problem of producing a new offering, and making the necessary deals to bring it to the market. Design takes into account multiple factors: the strategy and tactics, the terms of the sale and the deal, the ownership and distribution, the customer experience, and so forth.

Producers alter or redesign any and every aspect of bringing a product to market. They will tackle physical product design, product delivery, pricing, the business model, and the sales pitch. Perhaps just as important is the fact that they will design the ownership and deal structure to best fit the opportunity. Although they may be inserted into contested or mature markets, blockbuster ideas often manifest as products or services that the world has not seen before. Buyers will not be used to them, so Producers will need to engage in savvy salesmanship and deal making to put the proper foundations in place. Everything is on the table. For Producers, design *is* execution. Without their attention to the details of designing the blockbuster idea for the market, they are not likely to realize the same level of success.

This emphasis on design stood out for us largely because in most companies design is *inherited*—the business model, pricing, functions, sales pitch, deal structure, nearly everything is treated as predefined by the existing models, costs, and pricing that already exist in the company and/or the industry. If a company has a design sensibility at all, it applies almost exclusively to the sensory elements we typically associate with the word—the look, feel, or emotions associated with a product.

But when we examined the way that our study subjects went about the task of creating billion-dollar businesses we saw design everywhere, operating at multiple levels. The billionaire James Dyson, inventor of the vacuum cleaners and hand dryers that bear his name, literally designed his flagship product to be a better solution to home cleaning; *and* he designed the early pricing and delivery approaches to signal that his product was a high-end, high-tech option, closer to a robot than a broom.

Chip Wilson, the founder of Lululemon, was for years the chief designer of the clothing he stocked in his stores, inventor of the seamless yoga pants with a work(out)-to-play style that encouraged his customers to wear the clothes first to the studio and then for a coffee date with friends. The multipurpose fashion design let Lululemon design a high-end pricing model, charging upward of $100 for what would have been considered, in an earlier era, sweatpants. Wilson likewise designed the yoga-focused and meditation-centric culture of the business as well as the experiential environment in his retail locations—Lululemon stores keep only a limited number of items on the shelves to create the impression of high demand, and the art on the walls shows local yoga instructors teaching their classes at the elite studios of the region. Through these design decisions, Wilson signaled the kind of company he wanted to build and the kind of customer Lululemon wanted to target—fashionable, fit, active, local, affluent.[2] In Chapter 2 we mentioned the importance of empathy in conceiving the blockbuster. The same is true of its design—Chip Wilson could understand the boarding and surfing culture he targeted for Westbeach, but he is not a female yogi. Nonetheless, he could tap into the sensibility of the evolving urban "yoga chic" look that women were craving.

REDESIGNING MARKETS FOR BENEFITS AT SCALE

Self-made billionaire Eli Broad launched the home-building company Kaufman & Broad (now KB Home) with the intention of building traditional, single-family houses. But the business was structured from the beginning to pursue a design innovation: houses without basements, an insight that removed thousands from the cost of building.[3]

In the 1950s, when Broad started, gas heat had officially ousted coal as the home-heating medium of choice; basements were used for coal storage and had not yet become the "rec room" options they are today. No coal meant there was no immediate need for a basement. With that first design shift—followed by others such as open-plan ground floors and standard fixtures in kitchens and bathrooms— Broad was able within a matter of years to build hundreds of starter homes for up-and-coming families in the Detroit area. His approach beat out more established players that were, on the basis of their seniority, more beholden to the traditional ways of the industry.

Broad's empathetic insight into the growth of the housing market, and his Inventive Execution of a home-building business that pursued nontraditional home design, illustrates the role that design can play in the ability of Producers to execute an idea at scale. His first redesign of the affordable home allowed him to enter the market as an unknown and establish a foothold. Once established, Broad redesigned again, this time by focusing on the operating model of the home-building business.

As a trained accountant, Broad always had his eye on the balance sheet. He saw that the traditional business model of home building required developers to tie up a lot of capital to buy land that they then had to sit on for months or even years before they were ready to build, let alone sell. In this way, home builders operated like landowners. But Broad wanted to operate like a manufacturer, so he worked to redesign KB Home to streamline the building process down to just over a month, delivering only the materials needed to build the home in question and no more. He also shifted the payment terms so that he had cash from the buyer in hand to pay the contractor only after the house was finished, and bought only land he was prepared to immediately build on. These design tweaks gave him far more capital flexibility than competing players, and put him in a position to build a far larger number of houses with far less capital and fewer people.

Producers frequently operate in markets that require them to re-think the fundamentals of product or business design in order to deliver at scale. For example, when Sudanese native Mo Ibrahim began buying mobile licenses in Africa to create the telecommunications provider Celtel, he knew he would have to ditch the subscription pricing model that reigns in telecom.[4] Subscriptions are designed for salary earners, people with reliable, smooth incomes earned in consistent volumes at consistent intervals. They were a poor fit for the majority of people living in the countries of sub-Saharan Africa, where moderate to extreme poverty is common and incomes are "spiky." In fact, African governments were having difficulty wooing established telecom investors exactly *because* traditional players couldn't see how the impoverished population would be able to pay.

Where others saw a restriction, Ibrahim saw a design opportunity. Ibrahim bought licenses for a number of countries and engaged the World Bank as a funding partner to increase his leverage. He then set out to redesign the revenue structure for the poor customers who dominated the African mobile telecommunications market. His solution? Sell prepaid credit or scratch cards for a few dollars each. Even people living on a few dollars a day would be able to make the investment. The prepaid phone model is far more common now in a broad variety of markets, but Ibrahim was one of the first to do it. The large number of customers he converted to cell phone use helped keep minute costs low, and within five years Celtel was serving six million people in thirteen African countries.

In these examples, there is an inherent synergy between the design details that the Producers home in on, and the large-scale potential they are trying to unleash in the market. Both Broad and Ibrahim were building their businesses to cater to a much larger, at times less affluent, wave of customers than previous players had tried to accommodate. They paid close attention to the design details necessary to address the specific needs of a market of immense size. The changes were not aesthetic or even design for design's sake. Instead, they focused on easing the path to scale and attracting exactly those buyers who'd previously been shut out of the market by the high cost of ownership.

Consider what Broad and Ibrahim did in light of the more typical approach that businesses take when trying to attract a new segment. In most instances, companies take an existing product and then shift its pricing and functionality—for less affluent groups, they make the product cheaper and provide less. This inside-out approach focuses on what the business already has and how it can repackage it.[5]

On the other hand, Broad, Ibrahim, and other Producers using Inventive Execution manifestly do not do that. They reverse the equation. Instead of focusing from the inside out, they instead look at what the burgeoning customer group needs and design the business with that audience in mind. Over time, they reexamine and redesign, just as Broad readjusted his approach when he expanded to the California housing market, which is defined by high populations living in areas with limited land. His design solution, in that instance, was the town house.

Attending to design in this way can convert a previously niche market into a massive one. Micky Arison, the longtime CEO of Carnival Cruise Lines, and subsequently of Carnival Corporation & PLC, is an example of design thinking applied to re-create the cruising market.

Arison spent a good part of his youth at sea. When he was a teenager, his father owned a cruise ship. Arison went to work on the ship as a break after high school, and stayed for six months until his father pulled him off to go to college. Arison preferred the work, but his father wanted him to get an education.[6]

"I was getting too comfortable with it," Arison told us when we visited him in his offices in Miami. "I was going back and forth between school and work. But once you get into the ships you get hooked. I'm not the only one. If you look around our company, you'd see people thirty years, forty years with us. It's a business that people get very attached to. It's about providing an experience where people have a good time. It's about providing holidays, and so it's a business people really enjoy."

Despite the enjoyment there was a great deal of turmoil in those years. The relationship Arison's father had forged with a business partner soured and ended, and Carnival Cruise Lines was born from the rubble, run by the senior Arison, but partially owned by a holding company that sent a number two executive to oversee the investment. The number two reportedly felt that Arison junior should be given a more formal job, and thus he started moving through the different operational areas of the cruise business. From working as part of the check-in staff at the port to leading the reservations team in Miami, he learned the cruise business in the same way that Joe Mansueto learned about investing, or Chip Wilson learned about clothing retailing. It was a long-term, cumulative process that set him on the path to redesigning his industry.

Arison was busy learning and enjoying multiple aspects of the business when he was unexpectedly put in charge. "I was in my twenties when this was all going on. My focus was on learning and by twenty-six, twenty-seven years old I was running what today would be called the shore operation departments. And I didn't see it coming, but just after my thirtieth birthday, my father called me down to his office. We used to argue a lot, for whatever reason. I can't even honestly remember what the arguments were about. But we really saw things differently. And so at some point, he recognized that it wasn't going to work this way. So just after my thirtieth birthday, he called me down to his office and said, 'You know what? It's time for you to take over.' He took his briefcase and left and never came back."

The company had three ships at the time, and had signed a contract to build its first new cruise ship. The year was 1979 and the ship was delivered in 1982. That kind of slow, methodical growth reflected the vision put into place by his father, but it was not Micky Arison's vision. His idea was to redesign the niche cruising market into one with billion-dollar potential.

"There was a great belief in our company that we had a product that was different from what everybody else was doing. At that time, cruising was thought of as something for the elite. It was for wealthy retirees. It was not thought of as a mainstream vacation. And we really believed—I've used an automotive example—everybody in the industry was trying to be Lexus, Mercedes, and we were saying, 'You know, we want to be Chevy. We want to be available to every man.' And that's where we saw the great potential of size rather than having these boutique operations that only could service a small amount of people."

Arison began to expand the Carnival Cruise Lines brand through an aggressive shipbuilding program. By the late 1980s, Carnival

Cruise Lines had become the world's largest cruise brand. Arison then set his sights on a much bigger goal. The company went public in 1989, raising needed capital to pursue a plan for creating a diversified, multibrand portfolio of cruise lines catering to different market segments. "I wanted to grow more rapidly," Arison told us. "I thought there was a lot more opportunity. Even later after [my dad] left, as we were making acquisitions and growing, with each acquisition, he'd come and say, 'Do you really need to buy those guys? Do you really need that?' For each one, I said, 'Yeah, yeah.'"

Pausing here, we want to emphasize the fact that the distinction between Arison *Senior* (the company founder) and Arison *Junior* (the billionaire) lies not in Empathetic Imagination but in Inventive Execution. According to Micky, his dad had the same empathetic insight into the potential demand for the vacationing public. He agreed that the market could and would become much bigger. He just didn't want to be the one to do it. "He saw that," Arison told us. "He absolutely saw it as well, but at that time he was extremely conservative and the country was becoming very liberal. It was kind of opening up and he was old school, very old school." This contrast between the two Arisons shows how possessing one of the habits of mind is not enough without the others. It is not enough to have the vision of Empathetic Imagination without Patient Urgency and Inventive Execution to make the idea real.

Arison continued to grow the flagship Carnival Cruise Lines brand through new ship construction. He also focused on acquiring other brands, especially those dominant in other market segments as well as in other geographies. The Carnival parent today owns ten established cruising names, including Cunard, Holland America Line, Princess Cruises, Costa, and others. As Arison explains it, each deal required a unique design in order to determine the right pricing, ownership, and negotiation approach. Some companies had multiple owners, all of which had to accept a deal structure. Others had one owner, but the routes were less obviously profitable.

With a growing fleet of ships in place, Arison needed to also re-design certain aspects of the cruise business model in order to appeal to a larger population of the vacationing market. Branding certainly played a role, but Arison seemed to view brand marketing as a minor element of design. More important were the steps he, and others, took to redesign the business model and sales approach.

"Pricing was an issue," he said. "You need to get the price down to an affordable level, but also the packaging. In the early, early days Royal Caribbean started chartered programs from LA for cruises out of Miami. Everybody at the time thought they were crazy, but they would fill two 747s a week. And that really, really strengthened every-thing. Because [the market] was pretty much targeting the East Coast, and Royal Caribbean opened up the West Coast."

Arison quickly echoed the movements in the market to develop his company's air-sea packages, now an established concept in pack-age vacations. "We got our first deal with National Airlines, a Miami-based airline at the time. National Airlines flew out of eight cities in North America and that's how we started. At the time I was running reservations and trying to figure how do you do an air-sea package. We had no computers, we were doing everything manually. It was inter-esting trying to do that stuff, but we had fun. That was the other part of it—we always had fun. It was a fun job. People were having fun on the ships and we were having fun putting them on the ships."

Arison relinquished his role as CEO of Carnival Corporation in 2013 but continues to serve as chairman and remains very active in the company. "We merged ten years ago with P&O and Princess and we now have a significant percentage of the world market share," Ari-son told us of his current-day perspective. "We can't grow anymore from an acquisition point of view because we're not going to get any antitrust approvals. We tried to start a new cruise company in Ger-many and the German authorities said don't even bother applying. We're not going to let you do this." But these changing dynamics do not faze the self-made billionaire. He sees the challenges but he also believes the market has not yet reached its full potential. "I just believe in the concept," he told us, "the concept of a cruise vacation."

DESIGN INTEGRITY

Arison's belief in the concept that he spent his life growing offers an example of what we refer to as design integrity—a belief not only in the blockbuster idea, but in the necessary design foundations required to turn an idea into a real experience for the customer.

Howard Schultz's vision of Starbucks offers another example of design integrity at work. Walk into any Starbucks today and it is clear you are in a carefully designed environment. Each moment is choreographed, from the smell of ground coffee beans down to the placement of the coffee machines so that the baristas have to face the customers as they pull shots and steam milk and then set the finished espresso drinks on those pale wooden ministages.

In the early years of Schultz's tenure he made a lot of operational decisions to support his vision of Starbucks as a place where customers would want to linger. One important aspect is the service provided by the staff. Schultz was influenced by the community nature of the espresso bars he visited in Italy and the way the barista chatted with customers, often regulars, as he made their drinks. As part of his effort to replicate that experience in the United States, Schultz insisted that part-time employees be given decent health insurance. He believed it was the right thing to do, and it acted as a positive recruitment tool, attracting a higher-caliber, more committed employee than he might otherwise have found. Few other retailers offer these kinds of benefits for their workers, but it was part and parcel of Schultz's design, his vision of creating a warm, friendly service atmosphere in his stores—imagine the Starbucks experience with less committed employees.

Schultz insists on such design integrity even now, three decades after he purchased the small Seattle coffee roaster and turned it into one of the most recognized brands in the world.[7] So nonnegotiable is his integrity to the Starbucks experience that he made a costly decision in 2007 to remove a line of profitable breakfast sandwiches from the Starbucks menu for months during the most difficult period of the financial crisis. His reasoning? They were adulterating the Starbucks experience.[8]

Schultz writes in *Onward,* his book about steering Starbucks through a period of change, that the sandwiches were hugely popular. Alone, they upped the per-visitor spending rate significantly. But they corrupted the Starbucks experience in a number of ways, most egregiously through their smell. The sandwiches are served warm, and the employees had to heat them in a microwave. Inevitably, someone would leave a sandwich in a few seconds too long and cheese would melt on the microwave plate. On a busy morning no one has time to clean the plate before helping the next customer, so the cheese would stay and then burn when the next sandwich took its turn. The employees unwittingly removed one of the most important sensory triggers that signal to customers where they are and why. Starbucks became indistinguishable from the half a dozen other places defined by the acrid smell of burning cheese. Schultz preferred losing money over corrupting Starbucks, so he pulled the sandwiches and told the food designers to try again.

These examples reveal how pervasively design defines the experience and, by extension, the success of the product. Only through that close attention to the detail of the experience are Producers able to reach the thousands, even millions of customers who will embrace the product. Often, getting to those customers requires both a re-creation of the old ways of doing things and a concerted effort to help people reframe the way they think about what the product *is*. Producers show an outsized ability to design their products and the experience that feeds into the consumer's demands.

DESIGNING SALES, DESIGNING DEALS

When Philip Anschutz came of age, he joined his father in the uncertain business of oil-and-gas wildcatting in the United States. He spent a number of years acquiring leases and exploring them with only middling success, until he got a middle-of-the-night phone call in 1967, when he was twenty-seven years old, from the rig supervisor on one of his plots. He'd struck oil, a lot of it.

Anschutz reportedly went to the field and found it ankle deep in oil that had gushed out before the supervisor could cap the well. Anschutz quickly bought up as many of the surrounding leases as he could using thirty-day letters of credit, and immediately started drilling his investment. He'd struck liquid gold!

So it seemed, at least, until one of the workers accidentally set fire to the field. Anschutz was out of town when it happened and heard about it on the radio. Leveraged to the gills and desperate, he called Red Adair, the legendary oil-well firefighter, and asked him to put out the fire. Adair refused. The world of oil exploration was small and everyone knew Anschutz was in hock, Adair included. Anschutz begged and Adair eventually relented, but with a warning—he needed to get paid.

Fortunately, Adair was famous and Warner Bros. Studios was coincidentally planning a biopic of the firefighter starring John Wayne. Anschutz called the film production company and offered to sell them the rights to filming Adair dousing the fire. The two parties struck up a $100,000 deal. Adair got paid; Warner got prized footage to use in its 1968 film *Hellfighters;* and Anschutz got the cash he needed for his creditors as well as to pay Adair. It was an epic deal, and it set Anschutz on the path to becoming a billionaire.

Throughout this chapter, we have told stories of Producers designing products, experiences, and deals to bring their blockbuster ideas to the large markets they seek. Seeing a possible deal is an art form, as Philip Anschutz demonstrated in his ability to sell footage of a *burning* oil field. But as important as seeing the potential is the ability to design deals to complement the opportunity. From the negotiations that Mo Ibrahim conducted with the World Bank to give his telecom license bids credibility with the African governments he bought them from, to Micky Arison's deals to rapidly expand his cruising inventory, Producers bring creativity to the task, designing the deals necessary to bring their ideas to market, and then selling the deal to the partners and customers they need.

Producers are not necessarily born salesmen. But we do see many of them seeking to gain virtuoso salesmanship before they launch their billion-dollar businesses. Seventy-nine percent of the billionaires in our sample had direct sales experience, and the majority of them had their first sales experience before their thirtieth birthday. Forty-six percent of our sample began before they graduated from college, honing those sales skills with the proverbial lemonade stand or paper route: they may have sold Christmas cards, as did John Paul DeJoria, or soda and chips from their dorms rooms, as did Joe Mansueto.

These small ventures may seem childish, but for many such experience is formative. The act of standing in front of people and making a pitch inoculates them against performance anxiety. They learn that rejection is inevitable. Rejection is even productive—it teaches them resilience and allows them to hone the message and learn through experience that they have to knock on the next door to bring a sale. There is no real substitute for what sales experience teaches Producers about the customer and the needs they are trying to fulfill. For some, economically, there was no real alternative. Almost a quarter of our sample grew up in poor or impoverished circumstances (in contrast to half who were raised in privileged or affluent surroundings). John Paul DeJoria, the founder of John Paul Mitchell Systems and Patrón Spirits, was raised by a single mom in a poor household; he began selling to make some money to contribute to the family. Similarly, Kirk Kerkorian earned his pilot's license at the age of sixteen and started giving private rides and lessons because his family needed the extra income.

James Dyson, the designer and inventor responsible for the dual cyclone vacuum cleaner and the ubiquitous hands-free hand dryers, wrote of the years he spent after college selling a fiberglass sea vessel called the Sea Truck that he'd designed for the British manufacturing company Rotork: "It was time spent away from designing but it was to teach me, above all else, that only by trying to sell the thing you have made yourself, by dealing with customers' problems and the product's failings as they arise, can you really come to understand what you have done, to bond with your invention and to improve it. . . . I had to learn fast about selling, not because I was particularly interested in salesmanship per se, but because I wanted to make a triumph of this thing I had designed."[9]

We could include many more stories of how self-made billionaires gained sales experience, from Mark Cuban selling business software, to Richard Branson selling ad pages for the weekly newspaper the *Student*. But at some point for all the billionaires in our sample, there is an inflection point when the ability to grow and develop depends not on salesmanship alone, which we define as the ability to sell a known product or service, but on dealsmanship, which we see as closer to selling an idea, sometimes by reshaping the context of what is bought or sold, or by changing the product, the service, the terms, the conditions, or the risks. Dealsmanship, like product development, is about design.

Dealsmanship allows Producers to sell the products and services they already have, as well as set up the context and the relationships to sell the products and services they envision for the future. The latter is dependent on the former. Salesmanship is needed to make deals happen, but the deal needs the vision of a Producer who can design a business to make that next exponential leap of growth.

Tom Steyer's Selling and Dealing

The story of Tom Steyer, the billionaire founder of Farallon Capital Management, a San Francisco hedge fund, illustrates the Producer's skill with designing deals and then selling them to buyers. In his case, he adopted a nontraditional approach to investing for his sector, the kinds of investors he courted, and the people he recruited to work with him.

Steyer started Farallon in 1985, a time when hedge funds were viewed as investment vehicles for financial institutions and the extremely wealthy.[10] The pool of investors, already small, was even smaller after 1987, a year notable for significant losses and hedge fund closures. Investors were skittish, which is why Steyer seemed like someone they could work with. Even in 1987—his worst year— he did far better than most, earning a 6 percent return, which seemed like a fortune at a time when others had lost their entire investment.

Steyer made his name from his adherence to the philosophy of "absolute return," the practice of managing an asset for positive returns within a given period of time. Absolute return is more common now, but in 1987 funds were more commonly managed according to relative return, which is concerned with asset returns compared with an external benchmark, such as the market or an index. Absolute return was not a Steyer invention, but it was not common management practice when he started his fund. Likewise, Steyer's management of Farallon as an "event-driven" fund capitalizing on price inconsistencies after a major event, such as a merger, now is more commonly practiced, but it was unusual when he started.

As he described it to us when we met with him in his San Francisco offices, "Our way of doing absolute return was something that other people weren't trying to do, so it was needed. But now I've been doing this for twenty-seven years here. You can't do what we used to do, not because there was anything wrong with it, just because it's old hat. You can't sell a transistor radio on the street, either. It was time to move on, but we were definitely ahead of the curve for a long time."

Within a few years of starting Farallon, Steyer had developed a name for himself and his fund, enough to get the attention of David Swensen, chief investment officer at Yale University and manager of the Yale endowment. Swensen took over the endowment the same year that Steyer established Farallon and started almost immediately looking for nontraditional opportunities.[11] A student of modern portfolio theory, Swensen began looking for new investing options to balance the risk and optimize returns for the endowment. He was reportedly curious about hedge funds, and he talked to Steyer about his business when Farallon was still a very young fund (Steyer is a Yale alumnus and went to pitch Swensen while in New Haven for a Yale event). But Swensen remained reluctant, turned off by the compensation structure that allowed early hedge fund managers to make out big if they produced top returns, but share little of the pain if they lost an investor's money. Worse, Swensen worried that there were no incentives to fight for a better return. "The reason we don't want to do this, honestly, is in this format," Swensen reportedly told Steyer during a second meeting that took place in 1989. "If you lose money, you won't want to earn it back. You'll close down and start a new fund. That's the problem with the whole format."

That may have been the format for other institutions or in other times, but that is not the way Steyer works. Steyer talks a lot about investing and running businesses with integrity, a mind-set that dictates a lot of what he does, from the people he recruits, to the investors he courts, and the investments he makes. Money matters, but Steyer is famous for seeming impervious to its influence: he drives a well-used car and seems unconcerned about fashion or other trappings of wealth. He started his career at Goldman Sachs, and when he was leaving the Wall Street giant to start Farallon, his colleagues and seniors all warned that he was making a mistake. "They told me, 'You'll make more money here at Goldman Sachs than you will at any job you take.' And I said, 'I'm sure that's true. I'm not leaving for the money.' It wasn't about trying to get more money—I wasn't being cunning. I just didn't want to stay there." Doing a job that interested him and working with people he got along with was more important.

He told us, "I'm serious about being good. I really am. We are very serious about the excellence part. And we are very serious about how you treat people and how you treat each other and how you behave. We're trying to do a difficult thing in an excellent way and take a lot of pride in it, in an environment that often has a bunch of creeps in it. And some of them are really creepy. I mean, they've gotten in trouble for it. Obviously one of the big issues in this business is, if you're all about money, how interesting or valuable a person can you possibly be? It can be perverting. This can be like heroin for people. They're hooked on the reinforcement of making and having a bunch of money. And that's their feeling of positive self-worth. I say your net worth can't be your self-worth."

Swensen was eventually convinced that Steyer was building an honest business with strong relationships that he would do right by. That trust was reinforced by Steyer's commitment to take no management fees when his fund was down. Swensen invested $300 million in Farallon in 1990, which increased Steyer's assets under management by 30 percent, and made Yale one of the first university endowments to diversify its assets with hedge funds, now a far more common presence in the endowment portfolio.[12]

Producers do not expect to grow by repeatedly using the same tried-and-true approaches. Steyer's success selling a new pool of investors in Farallon and then managing those investments to high returns earned him a billion dollars. But his past approach to Inventive Execution won't carry his company into the future. "We have to do something that's very scary," he said of Farallon's future. "It's hard, but we need to be granular and effective around the world."

Steyer's current international focus has caused him to rethink and creatively design the deals he forges with Farallon employees. He told us, for example, about his efforts to find people in Japan and in Brazil whom he could work with—smart professionals with deep cultural understanding of the places where they work, as well as integrity and savvy about the way Farallon operates and the regulatory requirements of a fund domiciled in the United States. "We need what I have called sea turtles," Steyer said. "They can walk on the land. They can swim in the ocean."

Reportedly it took Steyer eight years to find the right person to work with in Japan and about as long for Brazil. "They've got to be comfortable in their country. They've got to understand our risk-reward philosophy and our need to be honest and our general culture." Given how rare this kind of person is, once found Steyer wants to keep him. To increase his odds he has designed compensation deals to make sure his employees feel invested. "They get a big slug of anything they do plus something from the center."

Steyer has gotten plenty of heat for that approach, but overall he thinks it works for Farallon; it makes team members feel appreciated and committed to the firm.

"One of my friends runs a hedge fund in New York," Steyer told us. "He's yelled at me for years: 'You're doing it wrong. It's not how you incent people. You're giving them too much of a share in what they do, blah, blah, blah.' He basically gave everybody a share in the firm. Of course, he gave himself by far the biggest slug of the firm. Everybody left. What we've always tried to say is we want to flow through the actual economics. So if you're creating value, we want to give you your share of what you actually created. Now you're going to get your share—not in the future. Eat what you kill. If you do it, you get it. This deal is not just about money. This is about being partners and working together and sharing the same values."

Steyer expects his deal making—with his investors and with his people—will see Farallon into the next era of growth, which will involve more presence in environments where the rules of engagement are less defined. "Say we want to go invest in Indonesia," he said as an example. "How do you do it? It's a famously corrupt society. So I look for excellence and integrity [in people I hire to work for Farallon in other countries]. Someone who is successful but honest. Because you got to ask yourself: How are you going to be effective in places that are not run by the League of Women Voters? There is no SEC oversight there, but there is SEC oversight of us. So that's hard. And doing it in a number of places and then having it tied in so that it's accurately organized and managed is hard. Very few people are doing that level of management."

The Role of Persuasion in Deal Making

The Producer's ability to sell a deal requires key skills in persuasion. Ibrahim has it, Anschutz has it, Steyer has it. Early experiences with sale making and deal making equip the Producer with the key tools of persuasion that she needs, especially as the deals get bigger and more elaborate. Many people assume these qualities are innate; that persuasion and its sister, charisma, are like blond hair or allergies, ingrained tendencies laid out in the DNA at birth. But the evidence suggests that like many other Producer skills, they can be learned.

Carl Hovland, a psychologist at Yale, first began studying the factors that allow people to be convinced of an idea in the 1940s and 1950s. Hovland had worked for the U.S. Army during World War II and had seen the way Adolf Hitler used mass media to elevate himself to demagogic status. The original model of persuasion that Hovland and his team came up with outlined three key phases to what the listener experiences as he or she listens to a set of content: attention, comprehension, and acceptance. For someone to sell an idea of any kind, the listener needs to pay attention to what is being said, needs to understand it, and needs to accept it into his way of thinking.

Only through the experience of working in the industry, understanding the interests of the person on the other side of the table,[13] and making a pitch and then making it again and again do Producers learn how to design a message that captures attention. As the experts advise in the negotiator's bible, *Getting to Yes,* Producers know how to structure their deals to their own advantage, and to make the pitch in a way that appeals to the interest of the other side. Audience is everything. A great pitch to the wrong crowd will go just as wrong as a bad pitch to the right one. The extensive sales experience that so many of the billionaires we studied have gave them the necessary ability to find the right audience and home in on a message that would not only capture attention but be simple and easily accepted into the listener's mind-set. The key lesson here is that Producers become skilled in the same way that top musicians get to Carnegie Hall—practice accumulated over many years.

Such acumen explains how Dietrich Mateschitz was able, as an unknown businessman, to persuade the young Formula 1 driver Gerhard Berger to walk around with a bottle of Red Bull in his hand without having an official endorsement contract. It explains how Steve

Jobs—the same man who had been ousted ten years earlier—was able to persuade the leaders of Apple not only to buy NeXT, a company with little in the way of unique technology, but also to reinstate him as Apple's CEO. And it offers some insight into the history of the Time Warner Center, the jewel in the crown of Stephen Ross's Related Companies portfolio.[14]

Redevelopment projects require a strong, name-brand tenant to anchor the deal. For that role Stephen Ross, the billionaire developer of New York's Time Warner Center, approached Dick Parsons, the CEO of Time Warner, whose offices had been in the Rockefeller Center area of New York's midtown. Parsons did not immediately warm to the idea, according to Ross. "Hey, Time Warner has three million square feet in the city," Parsons told him. "We've got thirty years to go here at 75 Rock. We don't need any space." Ross was undeterred. "Dick, this is not about space," he recalled saying. "It's about showcasing your company. Nobody knows who you are or what you are. They think you're part of NBC and you are the largest entertainment media company in the world. Look what's going on around the world. You need to showcase."

Ross's message resonated. "We talked for about two or three minutes," Ross recalled. "He said, 'I'll give you an answer in ten days and I will have board approval in sixty,'" Ross told us. "And that's how this deal was done." Ross changed the conversation away from what Time Warner had to what it needed—a way to present its name to an international public in association with a high-traffic, high-end, high-profile location. By focusing on his partner's interest, Ross was able to design and pitch a deal that appealed to everyone involved.[15]

Bloomberg's First Deal

Michael Bloomberg is most famous today as the post-9/11 mayor of New York City, but he began his career with the reputable Wall Street firm Salomon Brothers and quickly rose in the ranks until he was a rising star buying and selling blocks of stock sold by large institutions. But Bloomberg's star only shot so high at Salomon. He excelled as a trader, and he was made partner and then given responsibility for all equities. But in 1978, just as abruptly, he was demoted to run the information technology division of the company, where he was still stationed in 1981 when Salomon Brothers decided to merge with the commodity trading firm Phibro. Bloomberg was given a pat on the back and a severance check of $10 million. The company he'd worked for since graduating from Harvard Business School—the company he has said he would never have left—was letting him go.

Bloomberg was thirty-nine years old when this happened and couldn't imagine going to work for a different Wall Street firm. He took a chunk of the $10 million and created a business that merged the two skills he had developed at Salomon Brothers—knowledge of the securities and investment business, and of the technologies that assisted in the deals. "When it came to knowing the relative value of one security versus another, most of Wall Street in 1981 had pretty much remained where it was when I began as a clerk back in the mid-1960s: a bunch of guys using No. 2 pencils, chronicling the seat-of-the-pants guesses of too many bored trades,"[16] Bloomberg has written about the state of investment data at the time. Bloomberg imagined that he could build a system that took information about a mass of different investment types—stocks, bonds, currencies—and reveal a firm's position and show what was moving where so traders could see investment opportunities previously hidden by too much (and too inaccessible) data. Bloomberg hired four former Salomon people, including his Performer complement Tom Secunda, who wrote the first analytics programs, and got to work selling and dealing the as-yet-uninvented Bloomberg terminal.

Merrill Lynch's Capital Markets Division was the first prospect. As Bloomberg tells it, he went alone to a meeting with Ed Moriarty, the division head, and pitched the nonexistent product to him and his team as if it were established. When Bloomberg finished, Moriarty turned to Hank Alexander, the head of his software department, and asked his opinion. Alexander said he thought they should build it themselves—a not uncommon response in the "build it here" world of investment banking technology. When Moriarty asked how long it would take, Alexander reportedly said, "Well, if you don't give us anything new to do we'll be able to start in six months." With that opening, Bloomberg said, "I'll get it done in six months and if you don't like it, you don't have to pay for it."[17]

Bloomberg and his team had little more than an idea of what could help the traders at one of the country's most respected commercial banks. But he made a deal on that idea as if it existed already. Bloomberg used his persuasive capacity to sell the vision and then he went to work building a custom terminal that brought in proprietary data and analytics. "It wasn't elegant," he said of the first Bloomberg terminal they delivered. "It was laughably simplistic by today's standards. But we did it, and it worked."[18]

HOW EXECUTIVES CAN EMBRACE INVENTIVE EXECUTION

Throughout this chapter we have attempted to highlight the Inventive Execution approach self-made billionaires take to execute blockbuster ideas. Through fine-tuned attention to the details of designing products, customer experiences, and critical deals, our study subjects found ways to insert ideas built with Empathetic Imagination into large, expansive markets.

How can executives apply Inventive Execution to their own opportunities?

Take an Integrative Approach

First, look to integrate the various parts of the process involved in bringing a product or service to market. The typical organization is specialized, which means that the people who come up with the idea for a product eventually step off and turn their attention to the next idea, leaving other departments to decide how it will get built and sold. This specialization is manifestly not the Producer's way. On the contrary, Producers *want* to stay involved. They want to see their ideas actualized according to the vision they set out for them, without the compromises that inevitably take over when an idea touches too many hands that have too little invested in the original concept. We feel very strongly from doing this research and talking with billionaire Producers that the possession of *both* Empathetic Imagination and Inventive Execution is a defining characteristic of the way Producers work, and a source of their success.

What would happen if you integrated more of the pieces? As an example, what would happen if the James Dyson on your design team also had to spend a year trying to sell what he had built? How might the experience with selling change his designs? And how would his experience with design change the deals he seeks for the product?

In keeping with that integrative bent, what would happen if you gave your best deal makers influence over the design of the underlying product or business? Would your deal makers bring ideas around changing the pricing or the business model in a way that would open up new opportunities for scale?

We acknowledge that these suggestions may make a lot of readers nervous. It is instinctual—it even feels like a good idea—to keep your best thinkers thinking, and your best doers doing. That is exactly the right approach for Performers, but exactly wrong for Producers. Performers should be given responsibility for improving processes, for tackling and excelling on specific aspects of Inventive Execution.

Your Producers, in contrast, need to think *and* do—there is no separation for them. Organizations that want to capitalize on that integrative bent need to give their Producers opportunities to apply both skills.

Pilot, Pilot, Pilot

One way to give Producers opportunities to think *and* do is to embrace a pilot program. We noted in Chapter 3 that too many organizations spend far too much time planning for a product's release, and far too little time in the market with a prototype engaging directly with customers. If you want to act more like a Producer, embrace the pilot model of launching an early product in a limited market or with a hand-selected group of clients, and do this early and often. It can serve as a tool to test ideas and their design, and it allows Producers to practice Inventive Execution.

When deciding which products or services to invest in for a pilot program, make sure that Producers in your organization are making the decisions about which ideas to pursue. Ideally, those Producers will have concrete experience executing on ideas. Too often, design Performers give other design Performers most of the feedback, which can lead to insular "designer designs" that don't serve the customer. Having Producers weigh in can offer insights that the Performers haven't thought of. Having Producers also lead the product launch can pave the route to the sales and deals, and can even encourage pre-launch design adjustments that ease the path to scale.

Pilot projects are not without risk for the institution. We don't think they should be freebies for your Producers either. Yes, you are trying to encourage production, but you also want results. Therefore, you do need to measure how well your emergent Producers achieve Inventive Execution with the results included in the Producer's evaluation. Remember, the criteria for success are not the same ones you apply to Performers. You are not judging on the basis of incremental improvement but on value potential. Did the Producer execute in a way that substantially changed your market share? Did his Inventive Execution allow you to create or enter a completely new market in a different way? These are the terms of success.

Recruit with an Eye on Execution

The above suggestions apply largely to Producers you already have and have identified in the organization. For those organizations looking to augment their talent pool to include more Producers, look for individuals who have been involved in the design and sale of something completely new, or who bring inventive ideas to the table when you talk to them. These kinds of people can usually find inventive ideas about how to structure a deal, get access to resources, or get a project done. And remember that the vast majority of billionaire Producers have concrete sales experience. Salesmanship is almost a requirement to entry in this elite group. If your high potentials don't have sales experience coming in, make sure they get it quickly.

Finally, throughout your efforts, remember to celebrate. If there is a story of great Inventive Execution in your organization, broadcast it and make it a part of your culture.

5

REVERSING THE RISK EQUATION:
How Producers Avoid Risks Others Take and Take Risks Others Avoid

Far better it is to dare mighty things, to win glorious
triumphs, even though checkered by failure, than to take
rank with those poor spirits who neither enjoy much nor
suffer much, because they live in the gray twilight that
knows neither victory nor defeat.

—THEODORE ROOSEVELT

When she was twenty-seven years old, Yan Cheung used all of her savings—a sum of five thousand Hong Kong dollars—to start a Hong Kong–based paper-trading company that supplied paper pulp to manufacturers in mainland China. Five years later, in 1990, she abruptly shut down that growing business and moved to California to start over.[1]

Moving overseas looked like a huge risk. Mrs. Cheung spoke tentative English. She knew no one. Her list of local contacts was short, and the U.S. waste business was very insular.[2] Practically any outside observer would have called her decision to bet her entire savings—again—foolhardy. But within ten years, the paper-trading company she started in California, America Chung Nam, had become the leading paper exporter in the United States—and she was only just beginning.

Many observers of entrepreneurial behavior would look at this example and conclude that Mrs. Cheung had a large appetite for risk, but they would be wrong. Our research uncovered no evidence that Mrs. Cheung, or any of the self-made billionaires, took more, or more extreme, risks than the average individual. For every move Mrs. Cheung made that seemed, from the outside, to carry a lot of risk, there were many others who could be better defined as simply smart, even risk avoidant.

The cliché of the entrepreneur as risk taker is so ingrained in business culture that we expected our study subjects to reveal a lifelong love of risk taking. There were some outliers. Kirk Kerkorian had spent two and a half years during World War II delivering planes to Scotland on behalf of the Royal Canadian Air Force, flying them across a stretch of the North Atlantic where high winds and ice on the wings reportedly downed one in four pilots.[3] And there's Sir Richard Branson, founder of the Virgin Group of companies and as famous a sportsman as he is an entrepreneur. Branson once broke the record for crossing the Atlantic Ocean in a speedboat, and was the first person to make the same trip in a hot air balloon. He has also made numerous attempts to circumnavigate the globe by balloon, and has crashed—nearly dying—more than once.[4]

But these stories, colorful though they are, are exceptions. Far from out-of-control risk taking, we observed instead that Producers have the ability to take a Relative View of Risk: they are able to more reasonably assess what they stand to gain compared with what they might lose. When losses do occur, Producers have the personal resilience to recover and try again.

WHERE THE REAL RISK LIES

Taking the Relative View of Risk does not mean that billionaires eschew risks. It means instead that the risks they take are not any larger
than the risks present in everyday business transactions. More important, the real source of risk resides in other places than the average
professional would see them.

Risk is a matter of perception. This may seem like an uncontro-
versial statement, but viewing risk as a subjective rather than objective factor moves against economic orthodoxy—not to mention corporate
practice. The Nobel Prize winner Daniel Kahneman and his research
partner Amos Tversky first proposed the subjective nature of risk in a
1979 paper in which they describe a series of experiments they conducted to come up with their famous Prospect Theory, a model for human decision making. At its core, Prospect Theory argues that
individual perceptions of risk can be influenced by how an opportunity is framed, the context in which it is presented, personal experience, and other factors. Among other ideas, Prospect Theory first
introduced the world to the concept of loss aversion, the now-accepted
notion that people are more afraid of losing what they have than they
are eager to gain something new.[5]

For most people, the subjective nature of risk causes them to over-
estimate the risk of failure and underestimate the risk of missing out
on a gain. Producers, in contrast, have the ability to turn that tendency on its head. People like Yan Cheung are willing to risk failure.
If California didn't work out, she would just try something else. What
Producers are not willing to risk is the chance to capture an opportunity. This dynamic creates a critical duality between the *right* kind
of risk taking and the resilience needed to do it all over again when
the original plan doesn't work out.

A closer look at the context behind Mrs. Cheung's move to the

United States reveals the relative nature of the risks she faced. Apparently, she wasn't worried about how things would unfold in a foreign country. She *was* worried that staying in Hong Kong would threaten her livelihood. Hong Kong offered limited access to the resources needed to run her business, and China itself had limited materials from which to make strong, high-quality paper products. North America and Europe still had forests, as well as tree farms and reams of used material spilling out of homes and offices.

"If I'd stayed in Hong Kong I wouldn't have been able to satisfy the China demand. As at the time most of China's paper was imported, the market potential was vast, she has said."[6] So she moved to a place where the paper supply was unlimited and set up a company that exported raw materials to regions where the supply was meager.

Consider as well what she brought with her. Mrs. Cheung knew the market in China at a time when the nation was just beginning to open its economy to outside investors. She understood the demand for paper. She had connections with paper producers in China who would buy her pulp supply. She didn't speak English, but her soon-to-be husband and Performer business partner, Ming Chung Liu, did. And she had confidence in her ability to make the connections she needed to source her materials—she'd just finished building a successful business that did just that. Perhaps most important was her strong reputation. Paper is exported as pulp, which many exporters in Hong Kong in the 1980s watered down in order to increase output. Mrs. Cheung didn't water down her product. It was a point of pride for her, and her refusal to do it reportedly earned her threats from an organized crime syndicate with investments in her market. The least risky way to build the supply-side connections she needed to ride the huge and growing demand for paper in China was to go all in by moving somewhere with ample raw materials.

These details suggest that Yan Cheung's move was much less

risky than her alternatives. And yet, the fact that she faced less risk by moving was not obvious—if it had been, everyone would have done it. The ability to see the opportunity and understand where the real risk lay is at the heart of her Producer's perspective.

Not all bets pan out—even for Producers. Throughout the population of self-made billionaires we saw repeated experience with significant setbacks that would have moved many to abandon any dreams of entrepreneurial independence. Setbacks such as those experienced by Mark Cuban, who had to rebuild his first major business, MicroSolutions, after a secretary defrauded the company of its entire cash flow. Setbacks at the level experienced by the oil-and-gas magnate T. Boone Pickens, who was ousted from the business he'd spent decades building, Mesa Petroleum, in a scenario similar to that faced by the now-iconic Steve Jobs when he was removed from Apple.

The economists Richard Thaler and Eric Johnson have studied individuals who have suffered investment losses or business failures, and posit that the experience causes them to view future opportunities through a different, more pessimistic lens than they would otherwise. In the context of this chapter, past failure makes *most people* less able to take a relative view.[7] There are few things more anxiety provoking than the prospect of making a bad call that will cost you your job or your business. Producers nonetheless seem able to make the hard calls. When calls go wrong, they are able to dust off and start again. This ability requires not just capital but a level of personal fortitude and self-confidence that allows Producers to believe fully in the idea and in their ability to execute it.

Where does that confidence come from? When Yan Cheung talks about her history and her business, it is clear she has an accurate perspective about her own gifts and the challenges she will need to overcome. Back in the late 1980s, when she left for California, she didn't think she was going to fail, but if she had, it would have been far from the greatest challenge she'd faced in her life.

Mrs. Cheung was born in a coal-mining district in the far northeast of China, the oldest of eight children. Her father was imprisoned for three years when she was a child and the family did not have much money, which required Mrs. Cheung to start working early in life. While Mrs. Cheung was still a teenager, the family moved south to Guangdong Province. There she got her first job in business as a bookkeeper with a textile company. She used this experience as a launch pad to bigger companies and better jobs.[8] By that calculus, at twenty-seven she was already a seasoned businesswoman with nearly a decade of corporate experience. It seems no surprise, given her history, that she would feel confident in her abilities to make the right calls later on.

Yan Cheung's story is still unfolding, but she and Mr. Liu grew America Chung Nam through the 1990s by cultivating relationships with U.S. waste collection companies, garbage dump operators, and other sources of paper waste. Theirs is something of a road trip story—they bought a used Dodge Caravan and drove it around the United States cultivating relationships with potential suppliers and collecting materials. By 2001, America Chung Nam had become the leading exporter of paper materials. But by then it was only *part* of the Cheung empire. In 1996, while still building the paper materials supply in Los Angeles, Yan Cheung went back to China and set up a company called Nine Dragons with Mr. Liu and her brother. Among other activities, Nine Dragons owns paper-processing businesses that manufacture cardboard boxes.

The cyclicality is brilliant—America Chung Nam collects paper materials from the United States and sends them to Nine Dragons and other chinese paper processors, which convert the paper material into cardboard boxes. Inexpensive Chinese goods are then packed into the boxes and shipped to consumers in the United States, where the cycle starts again. America Chung Nam and Nine Dragons made Yan Cheung, Ming Chung Liu, and Mrs. Cheung's brother—an officer in the company—billionaires.[9]

In sum, for Mrs. Cheung, the real risk is losing the opportunity, not failing in the attempt. We see this perspective repeatedly across the billionaire population. Michael Bloomberg was not worried about failing when he launched his financial data publishing company mere months after his ouster from Salomon Brothers. He was worried, at the age of thirty-nine, about how he was going to spend the rest of his life.[10] Alex Spanos, now known as one of the largest developers of multifamily housing in the United States, wasn't worried about failing when at the age of twenty-seven he walked out of his father's bakery, where he had worked for his entire life. He was worried about missing out on the opportunities for expansion that his father was unwilling to take.[11] Carnival Cruise magnate Micky Arison was not worried about how he would run the sleepy four-ship cruise line that his father passed down to him. He was worried about reframing the cruise experience as a mainstream vacation.[12]

This perspective seems unique to billionaire Producers in part because it goes against the rules corporate employees have been trained to follow. For aspiring executives, the risk of failure costs them far more in terms of career prospects than the risk of missing an opportunity.

MORE EVIDENCE THAT BILLIONAIRES ARE NOT BIG RISK TAKERS

We were surprised, and somewhat skeptical, by our finding that billionaires do not possess a greater tolerance for risk than the average businessperson—the cliché of the entrepreneur as risk taker is so strong and pervasive in business culture. Yet as we thought about it more and did more research, it became clear that the issue is not risk tolerance but risk attitudes. Billionaires do not overweigh failure, nor do they take irrational risks.

One story that Dean Spanos, son of the billionaire Alex Spanos, shared with us when we sat down with him and his siblings in Stockton, California, underscores this idea of the kind of risks billionaires are—and are not—willing to take.

"We were interested in buying a savings and loan about twenty years ago in Florida," Dean Spanos began, "so Jerry Murphy, the CFO, and Dad and I flew to Florida and we went into this meeting where there was a conference table as long as the room filled with attorneys and investment bankers.

"We sat there for three and a half hours and listened to them talk about the structure of the company and the sale and everything. And I looked over at Jerry Murphy, who is a very, very, very bright guy, and I said, 'I really don't understand anything. Am I missing something?' Jerry says, 'No. I'm not sure I follow what they're talking about either.' So this goes on for three hours—and that's a long time for my dad—until the chairman looks at Dad and says, 'Well, Alex, what do you think? Are you interested? You think we can put this deal together?' And Dad says, 'I have one question. I asked that question three hours ago and I'll ask it again: Does this company make money or not? I'm talking about real, green bucks.'

"Nobody in that whole room would answer. So Dad gets up and says, 'When you can answer that question, give me a call; I might be interested.' And we walked out. Thirty days later, the savings and loan was taken over by the FDIC."

Alex Spanos was interested in buying a savings and loan, and this one was available and (as far as appearances went) operational. Plenty of successful businesses begin with the acquisition of a struggling company that the entrepreneur eventually turns around—Michael Jaharis did just that with Key Pharmaceuticals. The point of the story is not that Alex Spanos's risk radar prevented him from buying a struggling company but that he had a clear view in his mind of where the risk lay in the transaction and where it did not. Everyone in the room was talking about the structure of the company and the structure of the deal, but Alex Spanos wanted to know a simple fact: Does the company make money? That no one could, or would, answer was a red flag signaling that either this company was so complexly managed that no one knew for sure, or that management was hiding something.

The anecdote about Alex Spanos and the savings and loan deal that wasn't is representative of a "cut to the core" mind-set we have seen in many of the billionaires we studied. Walter Isaacson highlighted a similar quality in the way Steve Jobs negotiated contracts— he didn't want a hundred-page complex arrangement with this clause and that protection. He wanted simple agreements laid out in a few pages.[13]

Having an accurate sense of what will bring value and what will only bring risk is a truly rare skill in corporate environments. We have known companies that would willingly spend $500 million on an ERP software implementation (a high-risk prospect with unclear rewards) but fret over a few million dollars needed to launch a new product. Producers are simply better judges than the average person of where the real risk lies, and what the potential payoff might be.

We aren't the only ones having a hard time finding evidence to show that entrepreneurs are more willing risk takers. Michel Villette and Catherine Vuillermot, a sociologist and a historian, respectively, wrote a recent study on iconic business figures published as *From Predators to Icons*. In it, they argue that actions taken by business icons are often mistakenly labeled as high risk. Many "risky" deals, the authors argue, are better described as asymmetrical: The icon knew something about the value of an asset or the market that the person with whom he was doing business did not. In some instances, the icon owned another asset that could make a purchase more valuable.[14]

Villette and Vuillermot belong to a line of academic scholars investigating the relationship between entrepreneurship and risk. Among them is Robert Brockhaus, a professor of entrepreneurship at Saint Louis University. In 1980, Brockhaus published one of the first academic papers on entrepreneurs and risk taking. Even then, the received wisdom held that entrepreneurs are active risk takers. But when Brockhaus set out to compare the risk-taking propensities of people who started their own businesses with those of people who worked as managers in existing enterprises, he found no difference.[15] Other scholars have followed and have drawn the same conclusion.[16]

Morningstar founder Joe Mansueto confirmed what we observed in our research when we asked him about the risks he faced when he first started the mutual fund ratings company. Mansueto's own money was at risk—in the first few years he reportedly spent $250,000 of personal savings getting the company off the ground. To start Morningstar, he cashed in bonds his father had bought each month when Mansueto was a child. He was quite literally betting his nest egg. But to hear him talk about it, he wasn't really worried. "When I started I never felt risk," he said. "I knew at some level I could make this work. Worst case is my parents would take me in. I never felt I was embarking on a risky venture. It didn't take a lot of capital. I wasn't married. I didn't have a family or a mortgage. Thinking about risk and things not working out doesn't come naturally to me. I think more about growing a company. I am a builder. I believe the risks are manageable."[17]

MAINTAINING THE RELATIVE VIEW AFTER A SETBACK

Stephen Ross, the billionaire founder of the real estate development firm Related Companies, offers another case study in both resilience and the Relative View of Risk. Ross is no stranger to making big moves. Probably his best known project to date is the redevelopment of Columbus Circle in New York City, current home to the Time Warner Center. When Ross first began eyeing the parcel of land at the corner of Fifty-ninth Street and Broadway, it was a decrepit, highly trafficked, disorganized spot with ugly buildings and an outdated street design. Ross saw something different.[18]

When we met with him in his offices at the Time Warner Center, he reflected on what he saw in the area. "I looked out of my window and I said, 'Hey, you know, that is the best site in New York. Look at the exposure and all that.'" Stephen Ross envisioned what the site could become: a gateway to the Upper West Side featuring high-end shopping and mixed-use office, residential, and hotel space, with gourmet restaurants and a jazz venue prominently featured in a way worthy of its association with Lincoln Center, New York's famed performance hall and home to the Metropolitan Opera and the New York City Ballet. He said, "The economy wasn't there but I saw this as a world-class site and we wanted it." Today, the Time Warner Center is exactly the world-class site Ross imagined.

Ross seems to have always thought big, though he needed the right circumstances to pursue his big plans. When he was in his mid-twenties he relocated to New York from his native Detroit to work for the investment bank Laird, Inc. His job at the time was to structure affordable housing deals for clients seeking investments to use as tax shelters. But Ross had been in New York only a year when he lost his job in a leadership coup.

Ross quickly found a home in the real estate division at Bear Stearns, but there too he met with problems. Though Ross knew his market, he was too junior to close deals on his own. Real estate was a niche area of investment banking at the time and considered very high risk. Ross needed his boss at the table to make deals happen but, according to Ross, his boss treated him in a disrespectful and condescending manner. The situation eventually came to a head with a public confrontation between the two men, and Ross found himself again out of a job, twenty-nine years old and living in New York City, which was as lonely and expensive in the 1970s as it is today.

"Two jobs in a little over two years on Wall Street?" Ross mused when he told us about it. "With that track record, I'm not employable."

Starting a business is not risk free, of course. But Ross viewed his risks on the employment market as far greater than the ones he faced setting up his own real estate development business. Investment banking is a small world, and the real estate specialty is even smaller. A guy who has been ousted twice in two years is not going to land easily. He might have tried his luck, but Ross's assessment of himself as "unemployable" was right at least in the sense that a job at an existing Wall Street firm would shut him out of any meaningful opportunities.

He's not alone. Quite a few of our self-made billionaires had unstable experiences as employees—25 percent of those in our quantitative sample were fired or pushed out by an employer.[19] Steve Jobs had to work the night shift at Atari because his poor hygiene and petulant manner made the other employees complain.[20] Mark Cuban was a serial employee, moving from job to job every six months. He started his first business, MicroSolutions, at the age of twenty-five after getting fired for going on a sales call that his boss had forbidden him to attend.[21] John Paul DeJoria, the founder of John Paul Mitchell Systems and Patrón Spirits, got fired from both Redken Laboratories and the Institute of Trichology because of conflicts with a superior.[22] Michael Bloomberg was laid off from Salomon Brothers as part of acquisition fallout.[23]

An equally common experience for Producers within established firms is exemplified by that of the oil-and-gas magnate T. Boone Pickens, who wasn't so much an unsuccessful young employee as an unhappy one, annoyed and frustrated by the slow movement, waste, and lack of innovation he saw at Phillips Petroleum, his first postcollege employer.[24] Producers like the young Pickens are not necessarily pushed down or out of the companies where they worked, but they are chomping at the bit to have a bigger job, take a bigger opportunity, or negotiate a bigger deal. When it becomes clear to them that the firms they work for will not let them take those chances, they go out on their own. For these people, the risk of staying in an unhappy situation was far higher than the risk they faced working for themselves.

CONSIDER THE ALTERNATIVE

One way Producers look at risk is to negotiate their futures with a clear knowledge of their personal BATNA—the Best Alternative to a Negotiated Agreement, which was coined in *Getting to Yes*. Knowing the BATNA allows a negotiator to avoid the near-universal mistake of focusing on the deal itself, the internal complexities of which cloud the larger context.[25] In the case of Producers, the point of negotiation is how they will spend their time and how high they will go in their careers. They are less concerned about what they have to lose *now* and better able to assess what they have to gain from the opportunity in the future. Drawing again on the lessons from behavioral science, Producers seem overwhelmingly able to accept the risk of short-term loss or sacrifice in order to increase the odds of generating enormous value in the future.[26] Producers can take the relative view because they have a very clear understanding of the best alternative acceptable to them within that larger, more relative context.

For unsatisfied employees like Stephen Ross the best alternative they can see is working for a boss or a company who doesn't "get" them and who doesn't see the world and the opportunities it presents. At worst, they can be unemployed.

Having left Bear Stearns, Ross was already unemployed, so he had little to lose as he worked to create a business as a real estate developer. He had written up a business plan for a company while still with Laird, and he wondered if he could launch it. Ross was thinking big and using Empathetic Imagination based on his existing knowledge: he imagined a company that married all of the component parts of affordable housing development, including developing new properties, financing mortgages, syndicating existing developments, and obtaining government subsidies for housing and urban development. The challenge was that the development portion of the business required capital—a lot of it—and Ross didn't have any.

He had also seen the way the rapid business cycles of the 1970s and 1980s put a lot of pressure on real estate developers. While developers needed to develop new properties just to get the development fees, even a brief lull in demand could put their entire investment at risk. So Ross knew he urgently needed another source of income to provide the cash flow needed to ensure he could pay his bills while he worked on development deals. For that income he turned to syndication, which in real estate involves buying other people's developments and selling them to third-party investors. In his first year on his own, Ross managed to close three syndication deals and bring in $120,000—he had been making $25,000 a year on Wall Street. With each influx of money he pocketed only what he needed to live and put the rest of the cash back into the business.

Throughout the history of the Related Companies, Ross would lean on annuitized income sources for guaranteed cash. He started with syndication and added rental income once he had developed enough real estate to own his own properties. At more than one point those reliable sources served as a lifeline when he was faced with the possibility of severe business failure. He told us, for example, that during the 1991 real estate crash in the Northeast, as the result of the way he'd structured some deals he was left *personally* owing a number of banks $120 million. A competing developer then tried to acquire the debt from the banks and effectively wipe out Ross, but the coup was unsuccessful. The banks stuck with Ross and worked with him to structure a repayment arrangement, their faith firm in the slower, but still consistent cash flow the Related Companies enjoyed from its syndication and rental businesses. Within three years, Ross had paid back the banks.

Today, Ross's resilience, survival, and relative view have allowed his gaze to land on Hudson Yards, an audacious development initiative on the West Side of Manhattan, where Ross is currently the majority landowner among a number of development players. Several earlier attempts to finance the Hudson Yards project failed. Investors thought the plans too risky and too dependent upon the city of New York and the extension of subway lines by the perennially cash-strapped Metropolitan Transportation Authority, the operator of the city's public transportation system. Ross, however, has been patient and undeterred, his land rights acquisitions facilitated—if indirectly—by the advocacy of another self-made billionaire with a huge vested interest in seeing the Hudson Yards development happen: Michael Bloomberg.

Ross reflected on his ability to see what is possible and overcome when things don't go well. "When things are the worst you look for the positive," he explained. "Nothing goes straight up. You will always have times when you really have a major problem, something really goes wrong. You need to look and see where the positives are."

NEVER BET YOUR LAST PENNY

Though it is less flashy than the glamour and style of developments like the Time Warner Center and Hudson Yards, the syndication arm of Ross's business is a useful example of one of the ways we believe self-made billionaires put themselves in positions to maintain a relative view of the risks they face: they leave some resources available for the next year. Throughout the population of self-made billionaires we see them consistently engaging in the billionaire equivalent of shoving bills into the mattress. They invest big, but they often have a parallel spring of income or a safe source of cash they can count on to keep them solvent while they work the more exciting higher-stakes opportunities.

The parallel work can be pretty bland. When the Texas oil-and-gas billionaire T. Boone Pickens launched his first independent venture in the early 1950s, his sideline was well-site consulting work that paid $75 a day.[27] When Pickens left Phillips Petroleum, he was twenty-six years old with two children and a pregnant wife. In his view, his best prospects at Phillips would land him after twenty or thirty years with a vice president's position in exploration, a job he neither wanted nor was guaranteed to get—by his own estimation he was far from the best geologist in the company. Going out on his own looked remarkably better than staying to pursue an uncertain path about which he was lukewarm. He left to try his luck, but he knew he needed to put food on the table. Well-site work was grueling, but it kept money coming in while he worked on his maps and developed the relationships he needed to buy his first leases and form Mesa Petroleum, his first business.

Staying in a position to make the next investment is not quite the same as hedging your bets. Producers aren't setting up a source of income or investment specifically to balance another risky position. It is more like a philosophy or lifestyle approach with unique manifestations depending on the individual.

Alex Spanos, the construction billionaire who got his start by providing catering and housing for migrant farmworkers in California's Central Valley, operates according to a "cash-in cash-out" philosophy—even in the capital-intensive development business. Alexis Spanos Ruhl, one of Alex Spanos's daughters, told us that her father saw only one way to make any purchase, whether a car or a major land acquisition. "He would not buy something unless he paid cash for it," she said. "He was against debt. Against credit cards. He didn't like or believe in that. You want to buy something, you pay cash for it or you don't buy it. A lot of people didn't agree with that, still don't agree with that, but it works."

Mark Cuban's approach is not so different. He, too, advises young entrepreneurs to avoid debt and live simply so that the amount of money they need to get by is as low as possible. That changes one's perspective on risk while enabling a growing cushion against failure. "We each take our own path," Cuban has written, "but nothing short-cuts the dreams of a 22-year-old more than owing a shitload of money."[28]

Cuban likes to tell stories about his early postcollege days kicking around and trying to find his true calling. He slept on the floor of a friend's apartment, moved from job to job, and seemed to survive on bar wings and beer. He had a roommate well after he was financially stable and bringing in good money with MicroSolutions. These choices put him in the position, if the business collapsed, to start again.

He has had to use this cushion more than once. In the first two years that MicroSolutions was in business, Cuban and his business partner, Martin Woodall, had $85,000 stolen from them by their secretary—worse because it was their *only* $85,000. A few years later, his apartment burned down with everything he owned, including the $25,000 engagement ring he had just bought for his girlfriend. These experiences were clearly formative. Even today, the fifty-four-year-old billionaire sounds surprisingly conservative when he talks about building a business: "There are only two reasonable sources of capital for startup entrepreneurs: your own pocket and your customers' pockets."[29]

Staying in a position to make the next financial investment does not imply that Producers are not fully committed to their opportunities. They are. But for them, the definition of unreasonable risk is one that leaves them unable, in the event of failure, to dust off and start again.

REVISITING RESILIENCE

As we discussed in the early pages of this chapter, the ability to start again is necessary for breakthrough success. This is clear in the fact that the majority of self-made billionaires in our sample create huge value only with their second, third, or fourth business. Joe Mansueto with Morningstar, Mark Cuban with Broadcast.com, T. Boone Pickens with Boone Pickens Capital, Richard Branson with Virgin, Yan Cheung with America Chung Nam and Nine Dragons, Steve Jobs with Pixar, Steve Wynn with Wynn Resorts—all Producers mentioned in this chapter and dozens of others made their first billion after failure or moderate success with earlier ventures. Some of their preliminary ventures are tiny. Others are substantial, like Mirage Resorts, the Vegas real estate development business that Steve Wynn formed, grew, and was kicked out of in a 2000 takeover by Kirk Kerkorian.

Serial business creation seems to improve the survival prospects of a new venture. A recent study sponsored by the nonprofit Ewing Marion Kauffman Foundation shows that businesses started by serial entrepreneurs (in some cases with serial failures) were more likely to survive than those started by first timers.[30] In the world of risk, many Producers need these early ventures to acquire decision-making skills and get quick feedback about what is working and what isn't. That feedback is critical if an entrepreneur is to overcome biases about the real sources of risk to the business. Whether these early ventures are big or small, serial entrepreneurs learn through them about the vision needed to cultivate Empathetic Imagination, about the design skills and deal making critical for Inventive Execution, about how to operate with Patient Urgency. They also learn talent management, marketing, partnership, and so forth. These ventures are practice runs that give Producers the experience they need to take a Relative View of Risk. The fact that most organizations demote or eject people who fail is just one of the ways that companies hamstring their future value creation.

Yet we don't want to give the impression that it is easy to fail and then try again, especially not after spectacular failure at the scale experienced by Wynn, or by Steve Jobs when he was ousted from Apple, or by T. Boone Pickens when he was kicked out after almost forty years at the helm of Mesa Petroleum, the oil-and-gas company he founded. The year was 1996, and Pickens was sixty-eight years old and in the middle of a contentious divorce. He writes in his book, *The First Billion Is the Hardest,* that the times and circumstances dumped him into a deep depression.[31]

Boone Pickens was no stranger to difficult times. From a young age he had a clear view of his personal BATNA. "I got a job as a roughneck when I was sixteen," he told us when we sat down with him in his offices in Dallas. "And it was one of those jobs I knew there had to be something better than this somewhere. And then I worked for the railroad in '44, '45, '46; all summer jobs. And I was a boilermaker's helper, signal maintenance helper, and ended up a fireman on a switch engine, which is a guy who sits on the right of the engineer on the switch engine. And I thought, 'This is good training but what I'm doing is I'm seeing the jobs I'll have if I don't get an education, what I'm going to be doing the rest of my life.' And I thought, 'I'm not ready for this one or that one.'"

This fine sense of what he wanted for himself in fact served as the impetus behind Boone Pickens's decision to leave Phillips in his twenties and go out on his own, a path that eventually led him to form Mesa Petroleum with funding from two partners. The company grew incrementally at first by purchasing leases and prospecting for oil.

Mesa's leases produced well, which allowed it to buy more leases, and so on. Growth continued in this manner for about ten years, and Mesa developed a strong reputation. But by the mid-1960s, Boone Pickens began to see that the scale of the deals was severely constrained by Mesa's relatively small size. He had initiated an IPO a few years earlier in order to increase the company's access to capital and to buy out one of the two founding partners, but further growth would require a more aggressive approach.

Put in the context of the Relative View of Risk, Boone Pickens saw a far greater risk in trying to continue on a path of incremental growth—which might sound the death knell—than in taking the opportunity to do bigger deals. Boone Pickens chose the latter, and proposed that Mesa grow exponentially through the purchase of larger companies that possessed underpriced assets. Hugoton Production Company was to be the first deal.

"I had spent time studying Hugoton, a sleepy company which owned the majority of the rights to Hugoton Field [the country's largest natural gas field] in southwest Kansas. I looked at it and then I got to know the CEO of the company and another guy who ran the company. I went to my board of directors and I said, 'I think we'll be able to acquire this company.' I will never forget that one of [the board members] said, 'Boone, you don't have a snowball's chance in hell of getting this company. You're a dreamer and there isn't even a prospect for us to do that.'"

There was every reason for the board member to see the acquisition as impossible. Hugoton was twenty times the size of Mesa Petroleum. Furthermore, the CEO and head executive Boone Pickens had courted were not open to acquisition. But Boone Pickens found another way—he persuaded the board to let him offer Hugoton stockholders 1.8 shares of Mesa Petroleum stock for every one Hugoton Production Company share they were willing to sell. In this way, Mesa acquired 30 percent of Hugoton, and Boone Pickens began to earn a reputation as a corporate raider.[32]

The Hugoton acquisition paved the way for Mesa to become the oil-and-gas giant it remains today, but it was not without personal loss for T. Boone Pickens. The billionaire owned 23 percent of Mesa when he went after Hugoton. "If I'd been as smart as I am today I would've said to that board member, 'If I'm able to pull it off, I take no dilution.' But I didn't say that. We acquired them. They're twenty times our size. Now I have one-and-a-half percent."

Thirty years later T. Boone Pickens had worked his way back up to 7.5 percent of the company he founded, but it wasn't enough to protect himself from getting kicked out when he again found himself in opposition to other company leaders and the board.

Many at that point would have simply stopped working. Pickens didn't need the money. He'd earned nowhere near his first billion, but he had enough money to retire and live a comfortable life golfing and hanging out at the ranch. Yet he told us that the thought never occurred to him. He liked working then, and still continues now that he is in his eighties. Instead, he took five employees and a desk from Mesa and set up a new company, Boone Pickens Capital (known as BP Capital). His plan was to create an investment fund to trade oil-and-gas commodities. He planned to raise between $50 million and $100 million from old contacts and true believers, but the early days did not go as planned. First, he failed the National Futures Association exam he needed to become a commodity pool operator—twice. Then he had trouble raising the money he needed to launch. In the end, the fund went live with $37 million he managed to cobble together from a handful of trusting friends.

From bad to worse, by January 1999, the fund had plummeted to its last $2.7 million. Every investment the company made ended in a loss, topped off by a bad bet on deep-water oil drilling in the Gulf of

Mexico. Within two years, the BP Capital Energy Fund had lost 90 percent of its value and Pickens was staring down the barrel of another failure. "Don't worry," a friend and fund investor said to one of the BP Capital employees. "Boone will pull us out."

The friend proved prescient. While still at Mesa, Pickens had been pushing his board to invest more in natural gas reserves, motivated by the decrease in new oil discoveries in the United States. Now leading his own commodities fund, Pickens still believed that the price of gas would increase as demand from power plants and new buildings shifted to gas as a primary fuel for power and heat. Few shared his optimism, and the unmoving price of gas during the 1990s left Pickens on the losing side of that argument. But with BP Capital he got the timing right. In early 2000, Boone Pickens bought as many natural gas futures as he could with the $2.7 million he had left, and over the course of the year the price of gas skyrocketed, bringing the BP Capital Energy Fund up to $252 million in less than twelve months. He sold at the peak price of around $10 per cubic foot of gas and distributed $222 million to the investors. The next year Boone Pickens opened a second fund with a new idea cultivated from Empathetic Imagination, and was on his way to becoming a billionaire.

Today, Boone Pickens thinks far less about the low times he has faced throughout his career than he does about the wins he has earned. "There were sad days, bad days, scary days, all of that," he told us. "But those sort of fade in the past and you remember the good days not the bad days. What I did, it worked out right for me."

Compare Boone Pickens's resiliency to the hesitancy that affected Ron Wayne, an original partner in Apple Computer. Wayne had started a slot machine business that failed, swallowing $50,000 of savings. After that failure he went to work at Atari, where he met Steve Jobs. When Jobs later asked Wayne to join Apple Computer as a third partner to balance and adjudicate between Jobs and the engineering wunderkind Steve Wozniak, Wayne was initially enthusiastic. But then it became clear that they were going to structure the nascent Apple Computer as a partnership. Wayne, who was significantly older than his partners, was worried about the personal liability he would incur if all the borrowing and spending Jobs was doing to manufacture the Apple I at volume did not pan out. The fear overcame him and a few days after they filed the business paperwork he pulled out.[33]

HOW EXECUTIVES CAN LEARN TO REVERSE THE RISK EQUATION

Producers aren't knocked out of the entrepreneurial game by defeats—even those that seem entirely devastating. Mark Cuban likes to say, "You can try and fail a hundred times, but you only have to get it right once."[34] It would be hard to overstate how different those Producer actions and attitudes around risk are to the standard thinking within large businesses. Corporations talk about managing risk, but that can be a misnomer. Producers *manage* risk. Performers, and the corporations they work for, avoid it. Failure, in this context, is widely viewed as incompetent risk avoidance, with clear consequences for the tools that executives bring to their jobs.

The risk-avoidance perspective plays out in some proscribed ways in corporations, specifically as it applies to the pursuit of new opportunities. Standard corporate practice is to assign a high-potential employee to the challenge and see how she does. It's a way to vet that person's skills before elevating her to the next level. But if the process isn't managed carefully, that practice encourages high potentials to look only as far as the incremental win: get the new venture up and running; return a failing division to profitability; manage a change process.

Incremental wins are good and necessary—in some cases they

can even clear the way for a company to see an opportunity for Empathetic Imagination. But in too many corporations incremental is all there is. There is no blockbuster idea or pursuit driving the effort. As a result, the incremental wins are still wins, but they dead-end with themselves. They do not open up into anything larger, and even if they could, your performing high-potential employee has no reason or incentive to look for those possibilities. She knows she'll get the next gig if she proves herself; she also knows that any imaginative idea she comes up with is not likely to be led by her. Either she'll rotate to her next position before the idea begins to realize its potential, or it will be given to someone senior to her. She is not going to risk losing the low-risk incremental bump for the high-risk incremental bump, so she stays on the safe road.

And what if she fails? When a new product bombs, a new development costs too much to earn a profit, or a failing business unit cannot be turned around, the leader running it is blamed and either fired or demoted. The effect is at best neutral to a person's career, at worst completely destabilizing. The practice of punishing failure discourages leaders from taking the kinds of relative risks that can pay off, and it destroys the organization's ability to take advantage of that leader's resilience and apply her lessons to new ventures in the future. Professionals who have experienced failure are pushed out, and any learning they get from the experience is lost to the company.

The Producers we studied show a different way. Their view of risk, their resilience, and the benefits they gain from failure reveal how pursuing opportunities, testing new ideas, and iterative learning bring new value to the forefront. That value depends on the critical duality between a willingness and ability to look differently at the risks they face, and personal resilience to try again when the effort does not pan out.

In this book's introduction we explain that organizations will want to apply the lessons of each chapter to an ever-decreasing number of employees to help identify emerging Producers. Taking the Relative

View of Risk is a privilege afforded to only a small few. Only definite Producers should be given the leeway. Your pure Performers—no matter how skilled they are in their specific field—do not have the relative view needed to see where the real risk lies and make bets with high payoff potential. They don't have the Producer's skill of bringing together different resources to create new value.

With that perspective in mind, we recommend taking the following steps to reverse the risk equation in your organization.

Give Permission to Take Risks

When identifying emergent Producers you'd like to challenge with more responsibility, look at the range of risks they have taken in their lives and in their careers. Did they start a new line of business or service? Did they move to a new geographic location to extend or develop a market opportunity, or even to learn or explore something new? Ask them about it and listen to how they describe the experience. Did they view the effort as risky or as the logical, right approach given the circumstances? Did they see the real risks as lying elsewhere? If a prospect answers in the negative—no, I didn't feel the risk—and can offer a salient reason, you may have a Producer in your ranks.

Look for ways to challenge your talent. Give emergent Producers projects or roles that stretch their skills. The ones you think have huge potential should be given a chance to try out important roles that you aren't sure they can handle yet. You are not setting up anyone to fail. On the contrary, you are challenging them to succeed. When you give people something they have to reach for, their risk tolerance increases and you give them a chance to show themselves what they are capable of. Ideally, the Producers you challenge have either a proven track record or a palpable ability to see the upside—opportunities lost should be as salient to them as risks avoided.

When deciding who should get what role or opportunity, make sure as well that the managers and leaders evaluating the options also have the appropriate risk balance in mind. Performers in a leadership role who take an absolute view of the risks involved are going to be nervous about giving a chance to Producers whose risk perspectives are relative.

Beyond how you encourage individuals to expand their perspectives on risk, consider the culture of risk that exists within subgroups or functions in your organization, and work to make sure that the culture supports the relative view. Structure conversations about new opportunities to give the right time and weight to both the pros and the cons. Be careful to maintain balance—don't allow the concerns about risk to overrun the conversation. And keep in mind as you consider the risks that the billionaire Producers we studied are able to ask deeper questions about the real level of risk they face. Is the risk real? Is it likely? What is the material nature of the risk—if something went wrong would it put the entire business at risk or just the initiative that is exposed? What is the proportion between what the company might lose and what it could gain? Would the odds change if you had access to certain assets?

Question Your Automatic Risk Perceptions

As part of this practice of taking a balanced view of the risks, take the time to question your automatic assumptions—from both the individual view and the team view. Why do you think the way you do? When pursuing a new product, venture, or project, take the time to think through what path you want to instinctively follow and then pause and ask yourself *why*. Why do you want to go that way? Is it because it is the route with the greatest potential for Inventive Execution? Is it the route with the greatest in-house consensus? Is it the route with the least amount of risk? Is it the most obvious given your skills, capabilities, and resources?

The answers to those questions should tell you a lot about the opportunity and your approach to risk. If your plan of action has a great deal of consensus within the organization, for example, then you have good reason to suspect that you are pursuing an opportunity with only incremental value. Truly empathetically imaginative ideas will meet with resistance. And if your approach is chosen based on the fact that you have resources or skills that are widely available in your market, then you can feel confident that your route will be well traveled by others.

Humans like to think in terms of narrative, which is one reason scenario planning is such a powerful tool for strategists. The negative consequence of this tendency, however, is that we tend to slide down the same sluiceways in our thinking. The same "then" can frequently follow that one "if." You can dig a new channel by asking why and then match it with *what if? What if* we tried something else? *What if* the impossible actually transpired? "What if" is the Producer's path, the question that Stephen Ross asked about launching his own business, that Boone Pickens asked about the timing of natural gas investments, and that Steve Jobs asked when the artists at Pixar asked for more money to make animated films.

Shifting perspectives can also make clear that the sources of risk are not always obvious. Risk is a shape-shifter. Consider again Yan Cheung and her early business experiences as a useful thought exercise on the ways that risk can elude even skilled business minds. The "safe" move for Mrs. Cheung might have been to stay in Hong Kong and fight for dominance in that market. It is possible with that approach she might have thrived—she is a Producer, after all, able to see her possibilities where others see only a downward spiral. But arguably it would have been a much rockier path, marked by shrinking margins as she struggled to outbid competitors for the dwindling pulp supply, and watched as China sought alternative options. From that perspective, the low-risk low-reward approach that so many businesses embrace as key to incremental growth begins to resemble something closer to a corporate suicide pact, where incremental growth turns on a dime to incremental loss.

We by no means intend to minimize how hard it is to change risk perceptions. The habits of mind that cause people to take an absolute view of risk are legitimately difficult to break. It is not enough to *say* you should try to look at risk in a different way when you have been trained for your entire career in one approach.

This is one more reason leaders need to be selective about whom they cultivate to take the Relative View of Risk: Producers, really, are the ones who know how to use it. Performers, though skilled, are more likely to emerge from such an exercise with self-perception that resembles overconfidence—they are so used to excelling in their own area of expertise that they dramatically underestimate the amount of time and/or money it will take to realize a goal that requires multiple contributors with varying skills. This tendency is so ubiquitous in some areas that organizations have developed compensation systems for correcting such excess. The UK government, for example, has invested significant resources to understand and overcome the "mega-project performance paradox," whereby huge public-private projects—like the defunct luxury airliner Concorde and the eventually successful Sydney Opera House—are both very popular and overbudget (often by as much as 15,000 percent).[35]

Recruit for Difference

In addition to the work you do to challenge the talent you have and question the automatic ways of thinking that operate in your teams and groups, you should look to grow your organizations with Producers capable of challenging you to take the relative view. Make sure that you are hiring and promoting people who show capacity for Empathetic Imagination, Patient Urgency, Inventive Execution, and a Relative View of Risk. By definition, this is going to result in hiring high potentials who are different from the typical candidate that may have appealed to your organization in the past. Companies talk a lot about the importance of "cultural fit" in their recruiting, and we agree that culture is very important for corporate harmony. But culture can also become code for hiring people who all think alike. Recall that in the world of breakthrough value, consensus is more a warning sign than a signal of potential. When everyone in the organization agrees, you don't have enough people pushing the boundaries of what could be. Producers encourage important and productive tension and different thinking, along with some of the impatience that comes from their desire to make big ideas real.

So take advantage of it. Ask your Producers what they would do if you gave them 20 percent of their time to pursue breakthrough value. If a Producer has just finished one initiative and is at loose ends, ask him what he would like to do next for the firm. He may suggest a role for himself that doesn't yet exist, or ask to pursue a venture that is beyond what you already do. Listen to those suggestions and see what you can cull from them—they may lead to the next breakthrough.

Adopt a Learning Mentality Toward Failure

As a long-term effort, work on the environment you cultivate inside your team and in the organization. How do you handle failure? How do you tell stories about big opportunities that went bad? Do you celebrate the attempts, or construct narratives of warning about them?

It has become something of a life platitude to encourage people to embrace failure. There is even a whole catalog of clichés intended to value the attempt (no pain no gain, you miss every shot you don't take, and so on). It's in fashion today to *talk about* celebrating failure, but few firms of any size do it and almost no big firms do. We know of only one organization that makes a public event of it. In 2011, the World Bank hosted the first FAILFaire, a conference aimed at discussing major failures in the development community as a way for multilateral organizations, nonprofits, social enterprises, and others engaged in global development to learn and share lessons.

Businesses can afford to do more in-house to celebrate the good lessons inherent in any failure. Note that we say to "celebrate" lessons, not the failure itself—you don't want to make failure the goal. You are, however, trying to reframe useful failures as an outcome of thinking big and taking the right kinds of risks. It requires a nuanced view of when projects go wrong and why. Celebrate those that represent taking the right risks for the right reasons, and try to determine what might have turned things around.

6

THE PRODUCER-PERFORMER DUALITY:
How Producers Find Their Complement

The universe is a tension between novelty and habit,
and novelty is winning.
—TERENCE MCKENNA

John Paul DeJoria knows how to turn a good idea into a great business. The billionaire cofounder of John Paul Mitchell Systems and
the Patrón Spirits Company grew up in Los Angeles, and worked first
as a star salesman in the 1970s for Redken, and later in business development for Fermodyl and the Institute of Trichology. But his story at
all three companies ended the same way—he got fired. At Trichology,
he was reportedly let go because he was so successful at Inventive Execution, resulting in growing company sales, that his share of the profits made his take-home pay higher than the owner's.[1]

By 1980, he had left his job to start John Paul Mitchell Systems
with $500,000 promised from an outside investor. That money never
came in, leaving DeJoria unemployed, homeless, and living with his
young son in his car on the streets of Los Angeles. Paul Mitchell wasn't

much better off. Mitchell and DeJoria first met when the former was a high-performing hairstylist in London, earning accolades as the heir apparent to Vidal Sassoon. But times had changed. DeJoria and Mitchell had both fallen on hard times and they both needed a break, so they decided to make one together and start a business selling an innovative line of hair care products: a single-wash shampoo in an era when all the high-end brands were lather, rinse, *repeat,* and a leave-in conditioner that doubled as a styling agent. John Paul Mitchell Systems produced high-quality, salon-grade products designed to save stylists time *and* money because they needed only half as much product to achieve the same, or better, results.

The pair started with no money and arguably with no risk—because they had nothing to lose, the Relative View of Risk showed only an upside. An early investor getting cold feet left Mitchell and DeJoria with just $700 in start-up capital. Even with such meager beginnings, the two made a great team.

"He didn't do business and I didn't do hair," DeJoria said of his late partner when we sat down with him at his home in Austin, Texas. "Didn't have a clue about business. Paul was a great stylist. I was a businessman with a background in sales, marketing, and product development in the professional beauty industry."

With that division of labor, Mitchell performed, doing product demonstrations in salons to show potential customers how the products worked and how much less of it he needed. DeJoria, in turn, produced, displaying his skill in Inventive Execution by designing the business model of selling at a premium price exclusively in salons, and by proactively coaching salon owners on how to sell the products to the end client.

Mitchell's name recognition and Performer's skill set got the duo in the door with their early customers, but their survival is a testament to DeJoria's Producer's ability to design effective deals in spite of limits, a skill gleaned from a childhood of little and plenty of up-and-down times as a young adult—he'd had to borrow his half of the $700 in start-up funds from his mom. Because there wasn't much cash on hand, DeJoria arranged to pay the manufacturer upon receipt of product instead of in advance. That arrangement gave him a two-week head start, so that by the time the shipment arrived from the manufacturer he had the cash to pay for it. That the manufacturers were willing to accept the delay is a testament to DeJoria's dealsmanship.

Of that time, DeJoria said, "We knew we were going to be okay when we started being able to pay for the product on the day the invoice came due, and not two or three days later." The very survival of the business required the complementary contribution of a Performer's specific skill set and a Producer's business savvy.

THE DUALITY OF GREATNESS: A PRODUCER-PERFORMER MATCHUP

It may seem strange to discuss partnership in the final chapter of a book about the qualities that allow self-made billionaires to succeed. But we arrived here because the idea of the solo genius is so pervasive in the way people talk about and think about extraordinary success that it obscures the real story of how good ideas become great businesses.

The fact is that billionaires are overwhelmingly *not* alone. Producers have the Empathetic Imagination that allows them to see the potential for a new idea in the market, and they have the Inventive Execution necessary for the product to reach the greatest market potential. Performers, in turn, have extreme skills in one key area, but cannot usually see what *combinations* are necessary to convert a good idea into a great business. Creating billions in value requires both: the Producer's ability to bring together divergent ideas and resources into a blockbuster concept and inventive business design, *and* the Performer's ability to follow through on details needed to make the business work. The Producer and Performer are a pair of thinker/doers who complement each other, and integrate concept and action from Empathetic Imagination through Inventive Execution. While it is true that some Producers initially "pass" as Performers because the organizations that employ them force it, true Producers are not über-Performers and vice versa. Each needs the other to set the stage for massive value creation.

Thus the Producer's most important duality in fact may not be self-contained: it is the foundation built between individuals with complementary skills and mutual trust. In that partnership the Producer's greatest skills are amplified. She is able to focus on the pieces she is good at with the knowledge and trust that other necessary functions are also under control.

We have stated repeatedly that the ability to *see* an opportunity out of a mess of information is at its most basic level an act of the imagination. But inside organizations, the Producer is not always recognized as a creative, especially not in a traditional corporate environment, which tends to label employees as either thinkers or doers. Thirty-five years ago, DeJoria probably looked more like a sales "doer" who happened upon a thinker in the technical creativity of Mitchell. But Mitchell's ability with hair would not have been enough to lead John Paul Mitchell Systems to the level of success it has achieved without DeJoria's skill with the sale, inventive marketing, and his dedication to the salon channel. Mitchell would not have been able to get the company to the $5 million mark the two had originally set as the bar for success. The two made a perfect team, and each needed the other.

"Our goal was if we could only get to five million dollars a year in business, we'd each make a few hundred thousand dollars, we're set for life," DeJoria told us. "But it wasn't until we started growing and all of a sudden realizing that we were a million dollars, three million, five million dollars, wow, we could really build this thing big. Days before my partner died, he said, 'You know, JP, nothing would please me more than maybe one day we could do a hundred million dollars in business, even though I am not here.' I think at that time we were doing sixty million somewhat in that year, which was huge. And I said, 'Paul, it will happen. We'll definitely go over that.' And obviously we did. Considerably."

An important aspect of how these relationships play out is that they are conscious choices. Producers recognize that they need complementary skills if they are going to achieve their goals.

DeJoria touched specifically on this when he described the kinds of people he leans on to run his businesses. "You have to pick good people and let go. At Paul Mitchell, Luke Jacobellis, my president, is much better at details and following through on details than I am. Or my vice president of finance—I suck when it comes to details and administration. I understand it, but I'm not a bookkeeper. I need other people who can keep track of that. At Patrón, we had a vice president who should have been a president. In 2003 [when Martin Crowley, cofounder of Patrón, died], I suggested that this guy becomes president. He knows more than anybody else who's running the company right now. He should be president of the company, and at that point, Patrón was growing every year, but we really took off because Ed Brown was a much better president than I could ever be."

The "pick good people" piece is key to making these relationships work. DeJoria seems to have a knack for it. He said during our interview with him that he is often approached by people asking if there are any openings at Paul Mitchell or Patrón. His response? "Well, no. In fact, the big deal is we've only had maybe fifty people turn over at John Paul Mitchell Systems Corporate in thirty-five years. No one wants to leave. We have an environment where everyone gets to participate. If something is wrong, you tell somebody about it. And if that doesn't work, you tell me about it."

The Spanos children used almost the exact same words to describe the low turnover work environment that their father cultivated at AG Spanos Companies over the past thirty years. "Loyalty was number one without a question," said Michael Spanos, one of Alex Spanos's sons. Dean Spanos echoed this point: "That was the most important thing to him. He needed to be able to trust somebody implicitly. And they could trust him. We still have people that are working in our company thirty years and more to this day. I'm not talking four or five. I'm talking dozens. That trustworthiness was so important—he wanted your loyalty, and he also gave you his loyalty."

Alex Spanos's daughter Dea Spanos Berberian illustrated the point with an anecdote: "A secretary recently retired and she was here seventeen years. A few years ago she was having some financial problems—one of her grandchildren had health issues—and she was getting ready to resign because she needed a job that paid more. So one of the managers went to my dad and told him, and Dad goes, 'Why didn't somebody tell me?' That's how he used to talk. 'Why didn't somebody tell me?' And he goes down to the other end of the building to talk to her and he took care of whatever the situation was, and she stayed. That happened many times with the company. He stood behind his people and he was happy that he could do it."

THE PREVALENCE OF PRODUCER-PERFORMER PAIRS

More than half of the billionaires in our study sample started their businesses as part of a Producer-Performer team.[2] The number jumps to 60 percent when we remove financial industry billionaires from the sample.[3] Some famous examples include Steve Jobs (Producer) and Steve Wozniak (engineering Performer) of Apple; Nike's Bill Bowerman (Producer) and Phil Knight (Performer); and Amancio Ortega (Producer) and his first wife, Rosalia Mera (Performer), who together founded the apparel giant Zara.

The prominence of pairs among the billionaires we observed cuts against a lot of what we always *thought* we knew about how people feel productive and successful in their professional lives. Yet once we saw it in the data and began investigating its dynamics, the prominence of a Leadership Partnership began to make intuitive sense. Indeed, the concept resonates with almost everyone we talk to.

Outside of the billionaire population the Producer-Performer skill set works on a continuum, in which the distribution of individuals resembles a shifted bell curve (see Figure 6-1). There are few pure Performers and few pure Producers, but most of us skew to the Performer's side of the spectrum, partly because we are constitutionally inclined that way, and partly because our environments recognize and reward Performance. Academic Performers get all the scholarships and the rewards. Corporate Performers get the raises and promotions. This creates a cycle of performance in which corporate Performers are incrementally promoted until they are leading the company, and then they promote other Performers largely because they can recognize what performance looks like and reward it.

Figure 6-1: The Standard Distribution of Performers and Producers

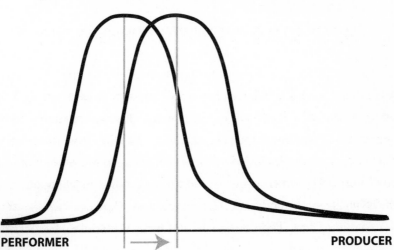

PERFORMER   PRODUCER

Left unchecked, this cycle breeds Performer's organizations composed of multiple functions that execute on their individual tasks exceptionally well, but with no integrative vision elevating those functions beyond the sum of their parts.

Breaking the cycle of performance requires the balance only a Producer can bring with his ability to hold on to multiple views at once—the imaginative and the empathetic; the urgent and the patient; the execution and the invention. Combining the Producer's tools with the Performer's expert execution creates the necessary ingredients for a breakthrough.

It's the combination that seems to create the chemical reaction needed to catalyze value. We note in the introduction the risks that corporations face when they get too specialized and componentized. Performers operating in their own silos rely on functional decomposition, whereby they break big problems into smaller and smaller pieces and then assign each person to do his part. This works so long as the market remains stable, its problems well defined and established. But creating new value in a highly contested market requires a new solution composed of several integrated, interlocking, and reinforcing innovations that together bring sustainable competitive advantage. John Paul Mitchell Systems, Broadcast.com, Carnival Cruise Lines, and dozens of other billionaire businesses reinvented their markets through the application of *multiple* important differentiators that allowed them to attain unique sustainable value. The Producer is needed to bring in the integrated view, and that view can become real much faster and can be more finely executed if a Performer contributes her specialty skills. Wozniak's engineering prowess made it possible for Apple to actualize Jobs's vision of what a PC for the everyman would look like; Paul Mitchell's history as a stylist made him uniquely qualified to know whether the products worked and what their advantages were.

Seeking and promoting a Producer-Performer Leadership Partnership requires, of course, a willing mind-set, which will admittedly require some work inside existing corporations. Most companies are hardwired to focus either on the individual—the master designer or the lead sales rep—or on teams—those five to thirty individuals working on a project. Yet given the centrality of pair bonds in most human societies, making the shift to pairs should seem intuitive. Two individuals working together, complementing each other, simply works better than other options. Multiple empirical studies on entrepreneurial dynamics dating back to the 1990s have shown that companies founded by "teams" (usually two or three individual founders) are more successful than those founded by a sole proprietor.[4] Within the billionaire population we studied, the Producer often has a long-term partnership with a Performer that brings out the best in both of them and makes massive value creation possible.

Figure 6-2: More Than Half of Self-made Billionaires Are Part of a Producer-Performer Pair

Ilitch/Ilitch
Cuban/Woodall
Malone/Barton
Gates/Ballmer Wilson/Day
Golisano/Angelidis & Chapman
Adelson/Chafetz
Ma/Tsai DeJoria/Mitchell
Spielberg/Katzenberg
Schultz/Olsen Hendricks/Hendricks
Bezos/Kaphan Lauren/Strom
Bloomberg/Secunda
Ellison/Miner & Oats Jaharis/Frost
Kerkorian/Yemenidjian
Geffen/Nyro   Resnick/Resnick
Pickens/Ross Bowerman/Knight
Gates/Allen Ortega/Mera
Zuckerman/Linde Simon/Simon
Jones/Scheiner Brin & Page/Schmidt
Soros/Rogers & Druckenmiller Winfrey/
Bren/Sim Blakely/Goldman Jacobs
Simons/Brown & Mercer Farrah/
Cook/Proulx Blank & Marcus
Wynn/Baldwin Anschutz/Leiweke
Ivanishvili/Malkin Broad/Kaufman
Peterson/Schwarzman

Leadership Partnership Pairs

Note: List of Producer-Performer pairs is not exhaustive.

Take Lynda and Stewart Resnick as an example. The Resnicks own Roll International, a holding company for the POM Wonderful, FIJI Water, and Teleflora brands, as well as for a volume of agricultural properties in the Central Valley of California. Lynda is the Producer, an advertising visionary with a golden touch when it comes to combining Empathetic Imagination with Inventive Execution—her particular skill lies in identifying a product with huge market potential and then finding the perfect marketing and strategy to capture the public imagination.

There was no commercial pomegranate juice before the Resnicks incidentally acquired a hundred acres of pomegranate trees as part of a larger purchase of pistachio orchards. Lynda had an empathetic insight and worked with a product development team to figure out a way to convert the pulp into juice and promote it to a buying public whose sole knowledge of the pomegranate likely stems from reading the Greek myth of Persephone in sixth grade. That a fruit associated with the queen of the dead is now widely viewed as an elixir of life is no small feat, a testament to Resnick's ability to see a market opportunity and attend to the details necessary to convert an idea into a market reality the customer suddenly cannot live without. Just as important, of course, is Stewart's single-minded performance with a balance sheet. "He's the one who makes sure the businesses are profitable," Lynda has said of her husband.[5] Stewart is in charge of finance and operations. While Lynda frets about the shape of the POM bottle and how it looks on the shelves next to other, taller products, Stewart makes sure those bottles get where they need to be and make a profit.

The cofounders of Little Caesars Pizza are another married Producer-Performer pair, though their roles are the reverse of Lynda and Stewart Resnick's.[6] In the heyday of the company, Producer Mike Ilitch was the playful creative who spent his day feeding his Empathetic Imagination. He alternately passed hours in the test kitchen cooking up new flavor pairings and in the halls of the marketing department, where he imagined new funny ads to complement the "Pizza Pizza" slogan that defined the company's promise to feed a family of four for less than $10. Marian Ilitch was the Performer, a self-taught accountant who managed the company's finances using a simple bookkeeping system she developed and maintained even when Little Caesars had become a $2 billion company.

We saw such pairings everywhere in the billionaire population. Two years after starting Spanx, founder and Producer Sara Blakely handed the operations of the business over to Performer CEO Laurie Ann Goldman, who ran the company for twelve years. Bloomberg's Producer Michael Bloomberg started the financial data giant with the technology Performer Tom Secunda at his side. In the technology world, these pairings are more public than elsewhere: there is Facebook's Mark Zuckerberg (Producer) and Sheryl Sandberg (Performer), eBay's Pierre Omidyar (Producer) and Meg Whitman (Performer), Microsoft's Bill Gates (Producer) and Paul Allen (Performer), just to name a few.

Sometimes these pairs seem destined to work together. The serial Producer Mark Cuban—cofounder of Broadcast.com and the current owner of the Dallas Mavericks—wrote about the Performer Martin Woodall, who was Cuban's partner in MicroSolutions, his first multimillion-dollar business: "While I covered my mistakes by throwing time and effort at the problem, Martin was so detail-oriented, he had to make sure things were perfect so there would never be any problems. We could drive each other crazy. He would give me incredible amounts of sh*t about how sloppy I was. I would give him the same amount back because he was so anal he was missing huge opportunities. We complemented each other perfectly. It would only be a matter of time before we both knew we had to be partners and work together instead of separately."[7]

In articulating the difference between himself and his partner,

Cuban highlights one of the key dualities—his perspective on risk. For him, getting a solution in the hands of a customer *fast* represented a far greater priority than delivering a *perfect* solution. Taking the time to make something perfect brought with it the unacceptable risk of losing out on the next opportunity. Cuban opted for fast knowing that the ever-changing nature of the 1980s computer industry was making almost everything obsolete before it was finished. There was no perfect.

When we sat down with Cuban, he clarified his perspective. "The way I defined it there's people that if you tell them to do A, B, and C, they're going to do A, B, and C. And they have no idea D, E, and F even exist. There's people that if you tell them to do A, B, and C, they'll tell you there's D, E, and F and will take the initiative. And then there's people like me that are bored with the first six letters and go right to G, H, and I. That's the way I've always looked at it. And so I've always tried to find people who complement my skill set. I always try to see what's next, where things are going. And I need people who balance that. And so Martin was as focused as they came, Todd Wagner [Cuban's partner at Broadcast.com] was as focused as they came. Smart, but completely different than me and as long as I trusted them, I didn't have to worry about A, B, and C getting done. And they trusted me to keep on pushing the envelope so today's A, B, and C were different than yesterday's A, B, and C, and different than tomorrow's A, B, and C. And I don't have to deal with the minutiae because I was horrible at it and to this day I'm horrible at it."

While these partnerships are necessary, the exact makeup of the Producer-Performer pair may change depending on the skills needed to take advantage of an opportunity. As Mark Cuban attests, the complement he needed for MicroSolutions was Martin Woodall, but the Broadcast.com dream team included Todd Wagner. Bill Gates started out with Paul Allen, but he also had a long-term Producer-Performer partnership with Steve Ballmer, during which Microsoft created most of its value. Jobs and Wozniak created the iconic computer maker, but Jobs and Jony Ive, Apple's chief designer, were the team behind the beauty and sensibility of the iMac, the iPod, the iPhone, and the iPad. John Paul DeJoria and Paul Mitchell founded John Paul Mitchell Systems, but years later DeJoria started another venture with his friend Martin Crowley, a talented architect who went bankrupt trying to make a business designing buildings.[8] DeJoria pointed him in a different direction and set him up as an architecture buyer supplying materials from Mexico for high-end renovations. During dinner one night, DeJoria asked Crowley to bring him some quality tequila from Jalisco—"the kind the aristocrats drink," DeJoria said, recalling the episode. The tequila Crowley brought back was "smoother than anything we could get here," DeJoria told us. DeJoria and Crowley went into business together, made the tequila smoother, and went to market the premium tequila brand Patrón, which today dominates tequila sales in the United States.

HOW IT WORKS: THE PRODUCER-PERFORMER EQUATION

What's the balance of activity between Producers and Performers? It naturally breaks down differently depending on the business and the opportunity. But from our research we see that the Producer discovers the vital need in the marketplace and creates the business design—and sometimes the product design—necessary to capture all the details of execution necessary to meet that need. The Performer applies the virtuoso creativity in operations or marketing or another specialty area necessary to fulfill the design's promise.

John Paul DeJoria, for example, saw the right business design that was necessary for Paul Mitchell's single-application shampoo product to gain the attention of hairdressers and the customers they served.

By selling exclusively in salons, DeJoria created a whole generation of hairdressers and salon owners who needed the product and acted as a powerful sales force for the brand. The product alone without DeJoria's distribution design and ability to execute would not be John Paul Mitchell Systems.

Likewise, DeJoria designed the Patrón business specifically to fill a gap in the spirits market. There was no high-end tequila available outside of Mexico before Patrón came on the scene. Signaling its quality required a premium price per bottle of around $40. DeJoria also gave it to friends—including celebrity chef Wolfgang Puck, whose endorsement helped pollinate Patrón throughout the fashionable bars and restaurants of L.A. Again, the product alone without the business design details and Inventive Execution would not be Patrón.

When we asked DeJoria how he would describe what he does compared with what his Performers do, he explained the relationship using an initiative he funds called Grow Appalachia as an example. Grow Appalachia is a project funded by the Peace, Love & Happiness Foundation that DeJoria started as a vehicle for his philanthropic giving (DeJoria has also taken the Giving Pledge, a commitment by the world's wealthiest people to give away large portions of their wealth in their lifetimes). The origins of the project date to 2009 when DeJoria decided to examine the range of philanthropic activity he engaged in.

"Here in the United States we're doing all kinds of things from saving the whales, to saving water, to helping the homeless become employed," he told us. "I asked around about other projects we could do to help people. A fellow that works for me comes from the hollows of Appalachia, and he said Appalachia's being neglected. So we did a little research and found there are a hundred and fifty thousand families receiving food stamps in Appalachia. So I thought I'm going to take that on. My goal will be in seven years to help at least fifty thousand families become self-sufficient and off of food stamps."

DeJoria is a businessman, not an expert in food scarcity, so he looked for a Leadership Partnership to manage the venture. He eventually decided to work with Berea College, an institute in eastern Kentucky. DeJoria funds the venture, Berea hosts Grow Appalachia, and Berea Performer David Cooke, a West Virginia native, holds the directorship of the venture.

"Here's what I wanted to do," said DeJoria. "Step number one was I would pay for seeds, fertilizer, equipment, as well as agricultural extension educators and volunteers to actually go out there and teach people how to farm. The goal of phase one was, you will feed yourself, your family, anyone destitute around you and be able to can for the winter so you can have food year-round. Phase two is you grow more vegetables—now you know you can do it—so you're taken care of, your family is taken care of. The extra you grow you can sell at farmer's markets or to local grocery stores as locally grown produce. Now you have some income, all right? Phase three is, once you have an income, teach someone else to do what you did. I'll buy the extra seeds and inputs and all that and you pass along what you learned to others. If I have fifty thousand families I could affect directly and each of them teach two others, that's a hundred and fifty thousand people getting to be self-sufficient and eventually making enough money off the gardening and the produce where they don't need the food stamps anymore."

Grow Appalachia launched officially in 2010. In its first year, the venture grew 120,000 pounds of food for more than 2,800 people. In the second year those numbers expanded, despite a difficult growing season, to 134,000 pounds of food for 3,694 people, and created a total of more than seventy full- and part-time jobs. In its third year, 2012, Grow Appalachia produced 320,000 pounds of produce for 9,000

people. From nothing to 320,000 pounds is an impressive feat, the result of Empathetic Imagination made real by a Producer who had the
original vision and a Performer collaborator with whom he is helping
him execute.[9]

"What I bring is the start of it," DeJoria said of the balance between production and performance. "I sometimes bring the finances,
the enthusiasm, and the direction to go into. I can do that pretty good,
yeah. And what a guy like David Cooke can do is they take it and they
execute it. In some cases they have the ability to do it and learn along
the way; in other cases you have to kind of remind them along the
way. Review things, make decisions with them and then you go forth.
In many cases they enhance my idea. 'Well, that's cool, but this even
worked better.' So it's kind of like giving the direction and follow
them through to make sure they are following that direction."

AN ABUNDANCE OF PRODUCERS

We have no doubt that when organizations skew too far in the direction of Performance—with no balancing Producer to integrate the
various skills and resources into a blockbuster idea—it becomes very
difficult to create massive breakthrough value. The most common
pairings we saw in the billionaire population were between Producers
and a Performer counterpart (or sometimes more than one) who had
a foundational role. There are, however, a number of great Leadership Partnerships between two Producers. Google founders Sergey
Brin and Larry Page are one example that started as a Producer-
Producer match that eventually found its Performer complement in
CEO Eric Schmidt. Theo and Karl Albrecht—fraternal founders of
the German grocery store Aldi—started as a Producer-Producer pair
until they decided for business reasons to split their company into

Aldi Nord (North) and Aldi Süd (South), each brother taking and producing with his half. Both Groupon founder Eric Lefkofsky and his partner Brad Keywell have Producer characteristics. Production is the necessary element—without it the business lacks the integrative view necessary to turn a good idea into a great business. Two Producers working together is the right match in some circumstances.

Herbert and Melvin Simon, cofounders of the Simon Property Group, demonstrate how two Producers can evolve and grow massive value. Their billionaire partnership is responsible for such innovative retail properties as the Mall of America in Bloomington, Minnesota, and the Forum Shops in Las Vegas. The former is still the largest indoor mall in the United States, and the first to integrate a shopping mall with an on-site amusement park as a way to bring a larger audience to the mall. The latter was one of the first efforts to integrate a high-end shopping property with a casino, in this case, with Caesar's Palace.

As Herbert Simon told us when we met with him at his offices in Indianapolis, the brothers traveled a long way to get to Las Vegas from the Bronx, where they grew up as the oldest and youngest sons in an immigrant Jewish family (Melvin Simon died in 2009).[10] Melvin enlisted in the army when he came of age, and found himself in Indianapolis when his tour of duty was over. He decided to stay and work for a local leasing agent there. Eight years separated the two, and when Herb Simon graduated from college and got married, Melvin persuaded his brother to join him and take a job with the same agent. After a few years the two left their employer to form their own retail development company.

In their family, being the oldest meant that Mel was responsible for his siblings (the third brother, Fred, came to the company a couple years later to head up the leasing division, and did so for many years before he retired). Perhaps it was Melvin's seniority, his famous charisma, or the fact that he had worked in real estate for years before his brother joined him, but Melvin took on the role of the Producer at the beginning. It was Melvin, according to Herb, who had the courage to suggest they develop their first properties, and it was Melvin's charismatic nature that got them the meetings and his savvy that allowed him to design the early deals that gave them the momentum to grow.

Their first developments were strip mall properties. Then, as now, retail is cyclical. The Simons needed a way to decrease the volatility of retail cycles, so Melvin hit on the idea of "anchoring" a property with long-term tenants with reliable business models. The concept of the anchor tenant is common today in retail. The obvious choice is a department store, such as Macy's or Bloomingdale's, or some other industry staple, but the unknown Simon brothers did not yet have the cachet, in 1960, to attract the attention of a high-caliber tenant. "Sears would not even talk to us," Herb Simon told us. To make their first properties successful they instead went after grocery store chains and pharmacies as anchor tenants. "Supermarkets, drugstores, the local chain supermarket," Herb Simon said. People will always need food, medicines, and personal care products, and the presence of those retailers kept a property more stable even if there was some turnover among clothing, housewares, or entertainment retailers.

"We were able to start doing that until we finally made our first breakthrough with Montgomery Ward," Herb said, "who was a little easier to deal with. But it took a long time. We had the right property and they wanted it. And it just evolved from that. They were easy to get to and we just happened to make the breakthrough with them and then shortly thereafter with [JC] Penney. Penney became a very big client of ours also. And slowly but surely we brought the mall to other department stores."

Herb credits Mel for those early successes. In fact, he insisted throughout our interview that the story he shared was really Melvin's story. But as he told us about the growth trajectory of the company and the nature of the business they were in, it was clear that Herb likewise took his opportunities to produce. When the company got to a certain size, the brothers no longer had the luxury of letting Mel produce while Herb performed. Instead they began to operate more independently, splitting developments so that Melvin produced half and Herb the other half. The brothers constantly exchanged ideas (and according to Herb, they disagreed and argued as well), and each relied on the other to serve as a sounding board and counterbalance. Though both Producers, they still benefited from the efficiency and collaboration that came from working intimately with someone with differing views and perspectives.

Through this collaboration they were able to address the challenges of a changing market. Even as the Simon brothers got their foothold in strip malls, the concept of the modern, enclosed mall was emerging. Herb Simon remembers the change as incremental. Slowly, the size and scope of the deals they did grew. "I didn't really stop to think about [how the modern megamall concept came up]," Herb said. "Based as we were in the Midwest, we had smaller cities and we had less grandiose plans because of the size of this marketplace. But as we got more involved with more opportunities and we got into larger markets, then it becomes more elaborate. And it's just an evolution that happens almost right under your eyes. Start with a supermarket and a drugstore and then the first mall with tile floors and rubber plants in the small little communities. And all of a sudden we had magnificent malls, live plants, beautiful terrazzo, and it just evolved. If you're in it long enough, you work hard enough, you get lucky. You got to get better. You can't stay the same. So, it's sort of organic. So, step-by-step, you sort of keep adding things that work and it keeps attracting more and more. And, you're involved in an industry where everyone was sharing ideas. You can't be the only one who has all the great ideas."

FINDING A MATCH

The self-awareness necessary to see the special skills in people and to know who can take on roles and do a better job is strong in the billionaire population. Consider Spanx founder Sara Blakely. Blakely worked solo for years. She had the empathetic insight that women everywhere, of all sizes, wanted a smooth line under their pants. She showed the patience and urgency needed to quickly work and rework the product, while dealing with repeated rejection from manufacturers and retailers. And she showed Inventive Execution in designing the product, the pricing, and making the sale. There was no separation between thinking up the idea and the design, and actively seeing the execution of her concept through all the way to the stores and into the buyers' shopping bags.

Today she still owns the brand she created, but she hasn't *run* the company in more than a decade. The change came arguably because her eye for Inventive Execution was so good that she blew out the capacity of her supply chain, an area where Blakely did not have particular skills or knowledge. This happened in 2003, when Blakely sent samples of Spanx to the self-made billionaire and U.S. talk-show queen Oprah Winfrey. Winfrey had once admitted to an audience of a million viewers that she routinely cut the feet off pantyhose to wear under fitted pants. Spanx seemed the perfect product for her, and they were—Winfrey listed Spanx as one of her favorite things of the year, unleashing a buying frenzy that challenged Blakely's small-scale production channel. Stock outages and missed deliveries almost cost Blakely the catapulting power of the Winfrey endorsement. Never again: that year Blakely hired Performer Laurie Ann Goldman, who collaborated with Blakely as the Spanx CEO until early 2014. Blakely continued honing her Empathetic Imagination, focusing on developing new product ideas and execution approaches, and acting as the face of Spanx.

CULTIVATING PRODUCER-PERFORMER PAIRS

Every day, businesses face new problems that require innovative solutions: solutions that require a differentiated view of the real risks the company faces; solutions that require urgent action coupled with patience as results unfold; solutions bred from equal parts Empathetic Imagination and Inventive Execution; solutions that require the business to do things it may never have done before. These are solutions that a Producer can see and that a Producer-Performer partnership can execute through a Leadership Partnership model.

Elevate Your Producers

Companies that embrace Leadership Partnership need known Producers in senior positions—people with a proven track record of seeing the problem differently from how others do, of coming up with imaginative solutions and ways to make them real. This may be harder for many than it sounds. We mentioned early in this chapter the tendency within large organizations to recognize and promote Performance. The problem-solving corollary to this phenomenon is that most problems are interpreted as needing a Performer's solution. As a result, even when an organization hires or keeps someone who is recognizably different in his views of risk and time, or in the degree of imagination be brings to his work, that person is only rarely given a project needing a Producer's mind-set and execution ability.

Unraveling the Performer's cycle will require many organizations to overcome their natural preference for performance. Performers are critical and necessary—Producers don't negate that value. On the contrary, the Performer's skills get stronger and his value is amplified, in the company of a Producer capable of seeing the combination resources needed to unlock value.

Though few organizations have an existing process for specifically identifying Producer-types in the organization, it has been our experience when we describe the Producer traits—Empathetic Imagination, Patient Urgency, Inventive Execution, and a Relative View of Risk—executives know right away who among their direct reports has Producer tendencies. If they are lucky, they may even be able to name someone who is off the charts. But while they know who has Producer potential, they often hesitate to put those people in charge of big new initiatives—because the Producer's way is so different from how Performers operate, taking such a step feels risky. Nor do managing executives think about how to match a Producer with a complement who has the Performer's ability to optimize within the boundaries of the Producer's design.

Seek Out Producer-Performer Pairs

Elevate your Producers, but also look for Performers you can pair with them to increase the likelihood of a breakthrough. Our research revealed that these pairs—and the occasional threesome—were highly effective at making value happen. Take a chance on them. It will require a shift in mind-set away from the traditional model of rewarding the individual or the team.

When it happens, acknowledge the Producer-Performer event. When a pair working together successfully ushers in a solution, recognize the chemistry of that pair making value happen, if even on a small scale. Don't break up that pair and promote each member individually. Producer-Performer pairs who excel together may find much of their alchemy in the *combination* of elements they bring to the table. Instead of splitting up that chemistry, keep the duo together and promote the two of them to the next challenge.

Get Out of the Way

Remove roadblocks that keep Producer-Performer ideas from moving up to the next level of execution. All companies have processes that new initiatives must go through before they go live. If a Producer-Performer pair presents a solution to a group of *Performers,* the odds of that solution being axed are much higher for all the same reasons that Performers promote Performers—they have trouble recognizing the value of production in action. Giving Producer-Performer pairs the best opportunities will require that they be evaluated by other Producer-Performer pairs.

Pursue Cultural Change

Elevating Producers, matching Producers with Performers, promoting pairs together, and setting up systems so that Producer-Performer pairs are judging Producer-Performer pairs will require changes in the organization. Having a Leadership Partnership model is a new way of operating, and the processes, actions, and resources needed to make it happen will take shape over time and through practice.

One step you can take to facilitate that change is to look at the talent and resources you have *already* to see whether you don't have elements of Leadership Partnership in action. Look, for example, for pairs who have worked together to bring about something new within the organization. Consider them—together—to lead a new opportunity that requires Production skills. If that pair has just come from a Production, make sure their next step is another higher-order Production—be careful you don't downgrade them to a role that requires only Performer skills.

Look also to the talent you acquire through your acquisitions. Sometimes you get the right feedstock through incidental means. To keep them, make sure those Producers are given opportunities to use their differentiating skills.

Think about what the organization values and how you communicate those values. In many, the stories of success that get promoted and repeated are Performer's stories. This reinforces the idea that only Performers can excel there. These dynamics are self-perpetuating. Your highest-potential employees are going to hear about your firm's "success stories," and those who want to stay will mimic the narratives they see those stories fulfill. Others—your Producers in particular—will look around at the success stories and be unable to recognize themselves. They will conclude that there is no place for them in your organization, and they will leave.

To counteract that tendency, make sure to celebrate stories that show Producers in action, applying their Relative View of Risk, Patient Urgency, Imagination Empathetic, and Inventive Execution. Even if your organization is just at the beginning of embracing Leadership Partnership, tell stories of Producer-Performer pairs in action to send a signal to emergent Producers—and their complements—that their way of thinking and a partnership route to success have a place in the organization.

CONCLUSION:
Creating the Billionaire Effect

There are those who look at things the way they are, and ask why? I dream of things that never were, and ask why not?

—ROBERT KENNEDY

We began this book by asking what might have been if the world's self-made billionaires had opted to stay at the large corporations that employed them early in their careers. But what might have been if those corporations operated in a way that made extreme Producers want to stay?

That is the question that we keep coming back to. The bulk of this book concentrates on helping you identify Producer behavior so that you can recognize it when you see it. The inevitable next piece is to know what to do with it when you find it. You need to know how to grow the number of Producers in your firm and how to motivate them to produce for you.

Imagine what British Telecom (BT) might have become in the late 1980s if it had followed the ideas of Mo Ibrahim, its onetime mobile engineer who was already pushing the coming rise of mobile telephony to his senior executives. What if BT had been less concerned about the erosion of its landline business, and more willing to have Ibrahim experiment early with a side unit or a subsidiary dedicated to commercial exploration of mobile telephony?

We believe strongly that great businesses like BT, Microsoft, GM, and dozens of others are led by Performers and are primarily hiring and rewarding Performers, unwittingly cultivating a Performer-centric culture. By definition, Performer centricity pushes out those people with the greatest ability to create breakthrough value. Hiring, cultivating, and keeping Producers will ultimately require changes to the way organizations think and act.

WHAT TO LOOK FOR

We have already described the career trajectory of a number of billionaires who started their jobs in established corporations. Though the experience of T. Boone Pickens at Phillips Petroleum was markedly different from that of John Paul DeJoria at Redken, we were struck by the fact that both Producers were originally given Performer roles by those employers: Pickens was looking for drilling sites through the same methods and approaches used by others in the industry; DeJoria was selling a known product through an established channel. (Curiously, DeJoria was applying Inventive Execution at Redken when he created a flat sales team with a few employees and outsold other regions that had multitudes more staff—an act which he claims got him fired.)

This observation held as we looked at the experiences of other Producers in corporate positions, and continued to hold as we looked around at the companies we work with, work in, and read about. As a rule, companies do a poor job of recognizing the differentiated nature of the talent they have. They likewise do a poor job of recognizing which roles require a Performer and which require a Producer. Put another way, they don't think through whether they need someone who is a master at executing in a known context or someone with the ability to apply new thinking in a new way to create new value. If your definition of professional excellence is Performer-driven, then all roles look like Performer roles.

The chapter on Producer-Performer pairs highlighted that corporations too often fail to recognize *after the fact* when a production has happened, and by extension they fail to see the alchemy of the Producer-Performer pair that made it happen. In that same vein, corporations rarely identify productions in the making and proactively seek a Producer to lead them as part of the strategy for optimizing the opportunity. When choosing leaders for a new project or initiative, few organizations concretely define the skills they need.

When your firm is trying to create a new product or service, do you default to giving the job to a proven Performer—someone known for leading an existing product line or service in a known space—or do you look for a Producer—someone who has created a new opportunity? If you have a once-dynamic division or company that has languished, slowly losing influence and value, do you place a Performer in charge to optimize sales of a proven commodity, or do you put a Producer in place to change what you are selling altogether? Do you see the latter as an option?

Bringing resources together in a new way requires a different mind-set and set of skills from scaling a known business. It requires Producers. We don't say that lightly, and we don't underestimate how difficult it is to choose a Producer over a Performer. Performers are safe bets. They think in ways that your executive leadership and your board will recognize. Their ideas carry authority as well as a high potential for consensus. They look like they will fit. And perhaps most important, high-profile organizations feel confident that if they make an offer, the Performer will accept it. None of those statements are true of Producers.

Perhaps for those reasons Performers dominate the short lists of the majority of executive searches. Look at the recent high-profile CEO transitions at Microsoft, Procter & Gamble, Apple, GM, Yahoo, Avon, and so on. Did any of those positions go to a Producer who is going to take them to the next level in a way that could not have been easily predicted? How will firms in the next five years think about re-placing seasoned veterans whose age or tenure may catalyze a switch? How might American Express and Disney and GE and Xerox ap-proach the challenge of replacing Kenneth Chenault, Bob Iger, Jeffrey Immelt, and Ursula Burns? Too often boards frame their options as a choice between one kind of Performer or another; they'd do better to frame it as a distinction between a Producer and a Performer.

Boards of directors, senior executives, and senior management need to understand the nature of the tasks that are planned for com-pany growth and health and make sure they have the right talent lead-ing them. Don't task a Performer with a Producer's role. And just as important, don't waste the Producers you have—the ones who rise naturally in the organization—in roles that could be and should be carried out by a high-quality Performer.

CALLING ALL PRODUCERS

At the risk of stating the obvious, being relentless about placing Pro-ducers in roles that require production skills is only possible when you have Producers available. Creating a resource pool of Producers in the organization requires two simultaneous and mutually reinforc-ing efforts. The first is to identify and cultivate Producer talent; the second is to shift the organizational culture, attitudes, and systems to be more Producer friendly, so that the Producers you have will stay and the Producers you want will come to produce for you. We have identified four ways to foster Producer talent in an existing organization: organic growth from within, catalyst hires, production partnerships, and mergers and acquisitions. Each of the four methods also has potential to cultivate a Producer-friendly environment. Let's examine each of the four modalities in turn.

Developing Producers from Within

Hiring, firing, and promoting talent is one of the most important mechanisms that organizations have to create Producer-friendly environments, but there are significant changes that most organizations will need to make to become Producer friendly. They will particularly need to attend to the way they recruit talent—both entry-level and experienced—and manage the talent they have.

First, an important clarification: You don't want everyone to stay. You don't want every hire you take a risk on to "work out." You don't want everyone to be a "good fit." So much of the talent management literature today talks about company culture and the costs of a bad hire. The result has been hiring managers looking for candidates who can "hit the ground running" and "fit well with the culture" and any number of clichés that in practice result in your organization continuing to do exactly what it has been doing in exactly the same ways it has been doing it. Those people who inherently fit are Performers, not Producers. Those who adjust themselves to fit may have had Producer tendencies that you squelched by sending a clear message of unwillingness to embrace deviance of any kind, positive or otherwise.

The reality is that Producers don't always fit. They think differently from others around them. The ideas they propose move against the standard approach you are following, and that friction is what you need to achieve breakthrough value. If you don't see some people leaving—frustrated because you still aren't moving fast enough— then you aren't pursuing enough Producer-friendly recruitment.

The inevitable turnover makes it all the more important to have a rich Producer channel. We are not suggesting that you abandon your established recruitment approaches. You still want the MBA from Wharton, but you also want to look beyond the typical profile you have sought in the past—perhaps the MBA starting a second career, or the person who worked for a start-up before pursuing a more traditional path. Whether the new associate has just walked in off a college campus or is the most seasoned and experienced executive, you want to identify and cultivate Producers as well as Performers.

For the young recruit or new employee, look for people whose résumés or backgrounds hint at a different point of view. Has that person created something new in her past—a new club that performed social outreach to the poor, or an on-campus venture to teach other students how to invest like private equity investors, or even an entrepreneurial initiative? Has that person followed a passion, whether through school, through travel, or through a job? Did he study a subject that is atypical for your organization, in the way Steve Jobs studied calligraphy at Reed College? Did she come up with a clever way to get something done—either in school, in her family, or in her life? By "done" we really mean *done,* even for young people. Ideas and enthusiasm do not make a Producer unless they come with the desire to see the idea manifest. Joe Mansueto, Morningstar's founder, said that he looks for follow-through in young recruits. The degree unfinished or the business idea unlaunched signals for him—especially if there is more than one abandoned milestone—that the raw materials of imagination are there, but without the fortitude necessary to work through the difficulty of execution.

Beyond recruitment, look to develop the young talent you already have in a way that gives people permission to show their Producer side. Perhaps give high-potential employees time to pursue an idea and see how they balance patience and urgency. Overall, you are looking to encourage your potential Producers to have new and different experiences, to expand their perspectives and to create greater potential for Empathetic Imagination and Inventive Execution.

As you create new opportunities for your potentials, take the time to examine your traditional reward and recognition systems. One of the most insidious things organizations can do is give potential Producers a production task without creating the incentives and systems that allow them to go big or go home. At PwC, we have had to face down our own inconsistencies in this area. We have had the experience of giving a latent Producer the opportunity to build revenue in an area that is new to the firm and have that Producer succeed, yet continue to evaluate her in the same pool of peers spending all of their time generating more traditional business.

We highlight this story not as an exercise in criticism, but to point out how easily getting only *some* of the process right can actually suppress production rather than unleash it. When you have a Producer who has shown the ability to produce at a small level, you have to decide either to invest enough to grow the business to scale, or to explain to the Producer why you aren't taking that step and shut it down. Don't allow a person with Producer potential to stay in the limbo of production. Senior management should not be complicit in this middle ground. Treating production with ambiguity sends as clear a message that the organization doesn't value it as preventing it in the first place. In response, extreme Producers leave, and latent Producers get the message that they won't be supported and just stick to performing— we're pretty sure the latter is worse.

Catalyst Hires

Catalyst hires are people you recruit specifically for a set of skills needed to pursue new growth or new capabilities. Every organization does at least some catalyst recruitment.

Catalyst hires allow some organizations to work around traditional thinking or bureaucratic structures that are difficult or impossible to fix. For example, USAID, the U.S. government's development agency, realized a few years ago that it needed direct access to innovative ideas and Inventive Execution if it was to have an impact on issues of global poverty. It is taking a bet on Michael Kremer, a Harvard professor and known Producer in the development space who has made his name as a renowned economist and public health expert.

Academia may seem like an odd place to find a Producer, but Kremer's status is inarguable. As a recently minted PhD in the early 1990s, Kremer's Empathetic Imagination allowed him to come up with a radical solution to the thorny problem of the way development aid is distributed. In the development world today, funders narrow in on a problem—say, student absenteeism in poor public schools—and give money for programs to address it. But their tools for determining if the program they supported actually helped, harmed, or did nothing at all are unreliable. As recently as ten years ago, development stakeholders had no real way to test whether solutions like free school lunches actually get kids into the classroom—just counting the number of kids before and after doesn't determine causality. And they definitely didn't know whether free lunches were better and cheaper than alternative programs, such as conditional cash transfers, deworming medications to reduce illness, or free uniforms.

Kremer saw a solution in the randomized controlled trial (RCT), the research method used by pharmaceutical companies to determine whether a drug is effective or not. Kremer was one of the first social scientists to design an RCT to test a social program, helping start a movement that has since become the gold standard in social research.[1] (As it turns out, school-based deworming programs are the cheapest and most effective way to get poor kids to go to school.)

Kremer is also one of the minds behind the Advanced Market Commitment, an important tool for catalyzing Empathetic Imagination in the pharmaceutical industry. An AMC is a commitment made by a large financier—usually a government—which promises to buy a certain quantity of vaccine or medication should a pharmaceutical company develop it. Advanced Market Commitments ensure a market for medications to treat diseases that disproportionately affect the poor in poor countries, whose governments would not necessarily have the funds to buy patented drugs. The idea, developed in partnership with Rachel Glennerster, an economist at MIT, with additional support, advocacy, and execution from the Center for Global Development, a Washington, D.C.–based think tank, converted an effectively dead area of pharmaceutical development into a field of renewed innovation.[2]

USAID is now betting on Kremer's producer habits of Empathetic Imagination and Inventive Execution to fight poverty. The agency hired Kremer and created Development Innovation Ventures, a division that is applying venture capital's staged-funding model to antipoverty innovation. DIV gives staged grants to organizations and individuals that are identifying, developing, testing (with RCTs), and scaling new ideas in an effort to prove which ideas work, are cost-effective, and have the potential to scale.[3]

Think about your organization: When you hire people to catalyze new growth and capability, do you look for Performers to execute on an existing business model or proven capacity, or are you looking for people who can move your business in new ways? If your organization is open to the latter, almost by definition catalyst recruitment may be one source of talent, because the process in many cases is more open to seeking people with different backgrounds or experiences.

As a consequence of our research on self-made billionaires, we have developed a set of questions we now use at PwC in interviews of certain catalyst recruits to assess them on each of the important Producer dimensions. We use these questions to discern whether a catalyst hire leans more to the Performer or to the Producer end of the spectrum. Again, this works best when we know what the task at hand requires— Producer vision or Performer execution. Example questions include:

▶ What are the most important trends in your industry, and what opportunities will that create for our clients?

▶ Have you ever creatively configured your execution of an idea to get it done faster, cheaper, differently?

▶ Have you ever experienced a real, smack-on-the-ground failure, and what did you learn from it?

▶ Can you describe an opportunity in your business that you are passionately interested in pursuing?

▶ Can you give an example of your track record of bringing ideas, people, and resources together in a new way to create new value, and making that idea manifest (not just talking about it)?

▶ If you were given 20 percent of your time to work on an idea or initiative, what would the idea be? How would you go about it?

The way you interpret the answers really depends on the context and the person you are talking to. A lot of it comes down to how passionately the person sees new opportunities and shows that he has delivered, and can continue to deliver, on them. We also can't overstate how much emphasis we put on resilience in the face of failure. We are not talking about faux failure, those stories that people with some experience in life whip out to articulate how they faced and overcame a challenge. We don't mean the class they earned a C in or the one quarter when they missed their sales targets. We are talking about real, affecting failures, the kind that make people take stock and reconsider their life and actions. People who have faced down real-life challenges know how to experience setbacks and get back up again with courage.

Producer recruits also need to be very self-contained. Leadership is lonely, especially while pursuing something truly new. You don't get regular positive feedback. If things go wrong, there is rarely someone there to share the heat with you. Successful Producers need to be sufficiently internally focused to operate for long periods motivated only by confidence that the idea is right and needs to become real.

And speaking of the idea—it probably goes without saying, but experienced Producer candidates will have them. Incremental ideas suggest performance; robust ideas production.

In the abstract, it may be difficult to imagine that Producers will just emerge from this line of inquiry, but our experience from applying the lessons of this book to catalyst recruitment is that the results are not ambiguous. You *know* when you have a Producer in the room.

We conducted an interview recently with a candidate whose Producer status was unmistakable. When asked about a business he would like to pursue, he outlined a consulting practice aimed at helping organizations manage the risks of damage to the electric grid. Over the course of a twenty-minute conversation, he explained his view that the current thrust of investment in smart meters and at-the-source energy use management was overemphasized (as he put it, a relatively small problem with relatively limited profit potential) and that the real opportunity centered around the aging utilities' infrastructure, grid damage caused by intensifying natural disasters, security concerns, and the risks that massive failure poses to all types of organizations— federal governments, local municipalities, insurance companies, as well as utilities, and other businesses. He had it all thought out, articulating what he saw as both the value proposition and the nearly limitless potential for scale—in a market like this, the city of Tokyo isn't going to care if you also help the city of New York.

We give this example less for the idea itself than to assert that there was no mistaking that this person had Producer qualities. He showed Empathetic Imagination by rejecting the typical narrative and having a viable alternative in which he saw business potential. He showed Patient Urgency in his assertion that the practice could and should start now and had a ten- to twenty-year growth horizon. And he displayed a taste for Inventive Execution as he articulated the business case and the model of delivery.

Develop Partnerships

Some companies will see a lot of success from their efforts to identify and develop the Producers and Producer-Performer pairs they have, and to develop catalyst initiatives to hire the talent they lack. Additionally, they will rekey the reward and recognition systems to celebrate production. Even with all those actions, however, some organizations may find they don't have enough Producers in their midst (and the ones they have may not carry them far enough). Those companies— and others who can't find and retain Producers, who want to experiment in noncore areas, or who want to move more quickly than is possible on their own—can partner with organizations that are engaged in Production, allowing their firms to grow in new ways.

There is precedent for this kind of strategic partnership. Throughout business history great innovators had interesting friends. J. P. Morgan was friendly with Nikola Tesla and even invested in the inventor's (ultimately failed) technology for transoceanic telecommunications. In that vein we see more corporate sponsorship of idea-generating platforms like TED and the World Economic Forum as a means to infuse new relationships and ideas into organizations.

Ford employees whose innovations lead to patents are rewarded with a three-month membership to TechShop, a seventeen-thousand-square-foot workshop in Detroit equipped with the machines and materials needed to tinker and build product or component prototypes. The membership program correlates with an increase in Ford patents filed, but the automaker sees greater benefit in giving tinkerers an opportunity to make ideas real and tangible—and therfore, harder to reject.[4]

There is a lot of variation in how businesses can use partnerships to foster production. Organizations may cultivate partnerships with universities, fund start-ups, acquire new companies but keep them separate from the core institution. They may also link more closely with suppliers, collaborate with customers, or incubate spin-offs as skunk works projects.

In these partnerships there is great potential to reconfigure combined resources into a new production. We see this potential in the recent partnership announcement between Coca-Cola and Green Mountain Coffee Roasters, owner of the Keurig platform. Green Mountain expects to launch a Keurig Cold machine for cold beverages in 2015. The world's cold beverage giant paid $1.25 billion for a 10 percent stake in Green Mountain, which gives Coca-Cola soda pods a prime position within Green Mountain's Keurig Cold drinks inventory—another way for Coke to be "within an arm's reach of desire."[5]

Other ventures may involve a mature organization in a tapped-out market taking a bet on a young, vibrant venture that can sidestep the larger organization's entrenched processes and approaches. In this way, an organization might seek to overcome its own limits by investing in a partner at the edge of thinking and implementation. This not only gives organizations an option in a new market, it also serves as another way for you to discover Producers in your organization—those with a long-standing interest in or commitment to an idea or a vector will gravitate to the new venture as a way to learn more and be involved in a way that is real.

Mergers and Acquisitions

Acquirers are clearly motivated by the desire to acquire resources, positioning in a new market, or the potential for scale. Sometimes, mergers are overtly about the people running the operation and their ability to pursue ideas.

The acquisition of Zappos by Amazon is an example of the Producer Jeff Bezos recognizing another Producer in CEO Tony Hsieh, and buying not only the business asset but the skills and vision of its leader. Warren Buffett, in contrast, could be said to be a Producer who has made his billions by acquiring cash flow in established, unchanging Performer industries. And the acquisition of Climate Corporation by the agricultural science firm Monsanto reads to us as an effort by a diversified agrigiant to grow Producer capability in an area with enormous potential.

Climate Corporation is a data analytics play in the agricultural space. Climate Corp analyzes climate and weather pattern data in order to provide farmers with information that can help optimize their yields by providing better predictions about weather, rainfall, and other climate events. Climate Corp data might suggest farmers plant ten days earlier than usual, or a week later. For Monsanto, which aims to help farmers feed the world using fewer resources and pollutants, the acquisition is a consistent extension of its goals via a route far outside its existing skill set.

Whatever the thrust of your merger, you want to keep the perspective that a portion of the value you acquire resides in the people—the founders, leaders, and business unit heads who have brought that institution to its current state. You can quickly gauge how friendly your firm is to Producers by observing how quickly the Producer talent—at all levels—leaves. In true mergers in which the acquired is subsumed into the parent, the top leadership is often the first out the door once their financial "lockups" expire. And what about the people one or two tiers down—the head of an important division or the executive in charge of business development? This may be where more Producer material resides, depending on the type and maturity of the company. When these people leave, they take a significant percentage of the merger's value with them. If they go on to start other businesses, you have wasted an opportunity to assign a Producer-appropriate tasks and have that acquired talent create value for your organization and shareholders.

Change the merger mentality. Too many mergers and acquisitions go forward with the view that the value lies in the market that business is targeting, not in the people behind the business. As a result, many acquirers look to shed human resources as quickly as possible. They look for overlap and redundancy. We are not saying that process is entirely wrong, but the speed with which these decisions are made almost ensures that the Producers get flushed out or take their opportunity to slip out with the crowd. Shift the viewpoint a little. If you are buying a company for the skills you don't have, look to see who the Producers are before you finish the deal, and make sure the incentives to stay are worth their while.

WHO GETS TO SAY NO?

We now turn to one of the thorniest problems that companies will face as they take steps to cultivate a Producer-friendly environment—who gets to say no? This chapter up to this point has focused on ways you can identify and cultivate Producers and production opportunities within and outside your business. But those efforts will only bring limited potential for a breakthrough if the powers that be stand in the way.

When identifying what is and is not a Producer task, or what is a production you want to be part of through partnership or in-house efforts, it is important to think through who is doing the judging. Leadership status, attitudes, and actions define whether your organization is Performer-centric or Producer friendly. If your most senior executives are Performers, and if they are hiring and promoting Performers into the most senior positions, giving green lights only to Performer initiatives, and generally manifesting the Performer cycle, they send a clear message to everyone in the organization that there is no room for deviance.

That's right—"deviance." We don't use the word casually. Producers *are* deviants, and production is deviant behavior. The results are marvelous, but there is no mistake that it moves—and should move—against the institutional grain in a way that will make Performers uncomfortable.

One example of this discomfort and its negative effects comes from an effort that has been getting a great deal of press in recent months: the self-driving car. Right now Google owns this space. Google is the brand that has been working on the technology, and there are Google leaders out there making it real in the marketplace and evangelizing its positive applications. Reportedly, the team that went to Sergey Brin and Larry Page for permission to work on the self-driving car was pushed to be *more* ambitious by the founding Producers—Page and Brin gave the development team the green light to make the car only if it would be able to travel a thousand miles in both highway and city contexts with limited GPS access, a challenge the car achieved in fifteen months.[6]

But Google's prominence in this market raises a thorny question: Why aren't leading car manufacturers pursuing that charge? OnStar, the in-car navigation system developed at GM with help from EDS and Hughes Electronics Systems (now DirecTV), has been around for almost twenty years and was for a long time the apparent owner of, for lack of a better word, the automotive "operating system" that many thought would become the platform for a lot of technological innovation, including self-driving capabilities. So what happened?

We suspect it comes back to leadership. Traditional organizations with Performers at the helm love taking faux bets on radical ideas, but when it comes to truly committing, they have trouble seeing the potential of disruptive technologies. They have difficulty with the idea that their innovations—historically built for proprietary use—might reside in a competitor's product; they can't or won't construct a narrative of change that shows employees, customers, and stakeholders the ways in which this new disruptive model is simply a natural evolution of what they have always done.

Compare the way the automotive industry has recused itself from Inventive Execution on the self-driving car with the way the Producer Bill Gates inserted Microsoft into the Internet space. In 1995, Gates knew Microsoft was late to the Internet party, and that Netscape, Sun Microsystems, and other competitors had already taken over and defined the browser and net server markets which served as the gateways to defining how users store, find, organize, and use information. In a letter he wrote to all Microsoft employees, Gates articulated his vision for why telecommunications mattered, why the Internet was at the center at that time of the new era of networked communications, and why the browser and other Web-enabling technologies were not *a* top priority but rather *the* top priority for Microsoft.[7] Gates sold his organization on the Web. It was Empathetic Imagination to see the shift in consumer demand, and Inventive Execution that began on the inside, a call to arms that Gates matched with important appointments and initiatives that allowed Microsoft to catch up and then surpass its competitors. Tellingly, there was no similar call to arms when Microsoft missed the new wave of mobile; Gates himself had already retired and moved on to focus his dual habits of mind on improving the lives of the world's poor.[8]

These stories of major change force corporations to ask themselves: What institutional means do we have at our disposal to make change happen?

We believe that the job of leadership in promoting a Producer-friendly culture is to put a wrapper of legitimacy around nontraditional activities. It requires a Bill Gates to explain why deviation from the former core of the business is consistent with what the company is about. Leaders need to point to deviant behavior and show the ways in which it is right, by highlighting how a Producer either got the firm into a new market, a new product area, or paved the way for a breakthrough. Commonly, leaders will need to provide "air cover" for deviants to take actions or pursue initiatives that are outside the norm. There are rules that Producers need to follow in this game. Leaders can't legitimize Producer activities that are happening in a way that goes against the values of the organization. Producers may be able to break the norms of behavior and thought in an organization, but there are ethical and legal standards that cannot be breached by anyone, no matter how great that person's potential.

The means to institutionalize Producers will vary depending on the inherent culture. Some will find ways to institutionalize a new production in a way that makes it seem incremental. This is a sophisticated dance that translates positive deviance into a form that is acceptable to and consistent with the organization.

However they go about it, corporations need Producers in high positions. They need people who have a vision for how the world is changing and a way to sell the company's role in it. An absolute requirement for the creation of Producer-friendly environments that recognize and reward positive deviance, that say yes to new ideas and strategies with disruptive potential, is the presence of one, two, maybe even a majority of Producers in the C-suite. There cannot be a compromise on that point. We have said repeatedly, and will continue to assert, that Performers are critical assets to the organization. But

Performers cannot construct the complex vision and see the combinations necessary to turn good ideas into great businesses. They are far more likely to ask *why* when the real question is *why not*. And they are far more likely to say no when the answer needs to be yes. You simply need Producers who are able to say yes, and you need to set up the organization so that Producers are the only ones who have the ultimate authority to say no.

The same goes for the makeup of the organization's board of directors. Even very powerful CEOs have independent boards that need to approve major decisions. The board can smooth the way for a production to take place, or it can put up roadblocks. To ensure it's the former, organizations need Producers in the boardroom, people who can recognize the intent behind new value-creating initiatives and even add value to their formation.

If you take this advice, you will be making decisions and promoting people with more of an eye toward building a Producer-friendly organization, but we are not saying that there will be no high-level Performers—there will be. Just as the Performer Luke Jacobellis runs the day-to-day operations at John Paul Mitchell Systems, and the Performer Martin Woodall ran the day-to-day at MicroSolutions, there will always be critical, irreplaceable roles for Performers because they are the ones who have the technical creativity to take a Producer's design and optimize the parts within it. The key is to elevate Performers with an eye toward Producer-Performer synergy.

REMOVING THE SHAME OF THE NEW

Being a Producer in a Performer-dominated organization requires an ability to deal with the shame of doing new things. Performer cultures can subtly shame potential Producers into silence, especially when a

Producer takes a risk or is given a chance to try something and it doesn't work out—wrong idea, wrong timing, wrong model, or any other wrong that causes an idea to fail. How would your organization treat a Producer who tried something new that bombed? If your honest answer is that you at some level shame him and others who try something big and fail, then you have work to do.

Across the business world there is a real shame component to being associated with a venture that doesn't take off or that has fully failed. Lessons from the self-made billionaires we interviewed make clear that failure is an inevitable hurdle on the path to success. Yet corporate environments often shame failure, and push those who fail into a holding pattern. These people don't get fired unless the failure is spectacular, but they are rarely given another production. Not all failures portent huge future wins, but some do, and at the very least those who try should be lauded for the attempt, and be allowed to integrate and even institutionalize the lessons so that the next effort goes that much better.

We view attitudes of shame toward failure as a symptom of the corporate tendency to eschew ambiguity. Nobody likes uncertainty, and corporations rarely tolerate it at all. The spreadsheets and earnings reports all serve to add a sheen of certainty to what is, at root, an uncertain world. And pursuing the truly new is the most uncertain activity businesses engage in. We are not suggesting that businesses embrace ambiguity—that would be overstating it. But there does need to be some heightened tolerance of it for productions whose outcomes are radically uncertain but potentially huge. The examples of Inventive Execution we highlighted in Chapter 4 show the myriad ways that a Producer, in the process of making an idea real, must design, adjust, and rejigger business models to find the right fit. Producers may get it wrong before they get it right. They need to be allowed some leeway for those mistakes to happen.

And when a venture has passed from ambiguous to definite

failure? Cut it off. Don't keep the project and its Producer in limbo. An effort that earns profits but isn't big enough to earn institutional attention should be addressed with the same definitive action as one that is clearly never going to earn. "The signs are all there," Groupon founder Eric Lefkofsky said of the success prospects of the ventures he supports. "And 99.9 percent of the time the signs are not wrong."

NURTURE PRODUCERS: WHERE SERENDIPITY MEETS INTENT

In our study of billionaires we looked at the outliers. These people work neither in the box nor outside the box. They make new boxes. The job of the leader is to walk the line between the new boxes built by Producers and the proscribed boxes process-engineered by Performers, accepting both and rejecting neither. Leaders need to be open to finding and supporting positive deviance while also pushing for systematic improvement.

Just as the billionaires have important habits of mind, we encourage senior leaders to develop new habits of mind focused on finding, encouraging, rewarding, and partnering to augment their Producer talent pool. But it's not a cookbook. There is no fail-safe recipe that will result every time in high-value production. Throughout the book we have suggested ideas and approaches that we have seen create extreme Producers and establish an environment that will attract and foster them. But inherent in these pieces of advice is a strong belief that miracles cannot be manufactured. As shown in the diversity of stories told in the book, great Producers come from odd places. Their presence may be unexpected. Serendipity is as much a factor in greatness as planning. Each organization—each leader—will have to follow its own opportunities as they arise. True Producer leadership is the act of being aware of and open to the miracles that happen naturally, and to escape the natural tendency to try to manufacture them. Trying to manufacture a miracle is like trying to explain a joke—it dies in the process of dissection.

The key imperative for management is to differentiate between opportunities that need a Performer and those that need a Producer. Look at areas of achievement for the business and at who did the work. When it is a Producer, recognize that and give that Producer her next Producer-appropriate challenge. The management team that hires more Producers and is more attuned to supporting them is more likely to achieve the balance of talent necessary for a breakthrough. The market economy delivers extreme returns; when you have extreme Producers, the value will flow to those leaders who can nurture this talent pool better than others.

ACKNOWLEDGMENTS

Seeds of inspiration came from colleagues who believed in a fine idea long before it became a project. The notion of a Producer came from extensive conversations and a presentation at our PwC Exchange by a dear friend and Producer, Kevin Hartley. A source of constant inspiration, Kevin is busy creating amazing new billion-dollar hit products in his own career.

Among our PwC partners, Adam Gutstein, our longtime colleague and friend, believed in the project early on, and Joe Duffy not only urged us on, but found the budget for the project—he's a great partner in every sense of the word.

Once the concept and budget were in place, four people proved critical to this book: Kate Barnard, Abby Brennan, Tim Ogden, and Laura Starita.

PwC colleagues Kate and Abby led the book's research effort. They located and organized a vast amount of unwieldy, hard-to-find information and managed research teams. Their work provided the foundation for our narrative. Kate and Abby also deftly navigated relationships with other partners across the firm and helped us gain access to a number of the billionaires we interviewed. They epitomize what we look for in young professionals at PwC.

Tim Ogden and Laura Starita, respectively the executive partner and managing partner of the communications firm Sona Partners, are themselves a great founding duo. Their mission is to explore "ideas that matter," and they live up to it. We always knew that we were dealing with not simply fellow writers but thinking partners who had the courage and patience to delve into the ideas, roll them around in the baths of data, compare them with other relevant research, and take the time to get both the thinking and the argument right.

Augmenting the core team of Kate, Abby, Tim, and Laura was Helen Poot of PwC's Research and Analytics group. Helen helped us profile the billionaires who appear in this book—all 120 of them; and she was consistently prompt, thorough, and ready for any request.

The stars of this book are, of course, the self-made billionaires we studied, in particular the sixteen who took the time to share their stories directly with us. We appreciate their openness and their generosity with their time as well as their enthusiasm for our quest.

To obtain access to them, we drew upon the relationships of many individuals, both colleagues and friends. John reached out to Tom Steyer, a fellow student from the Phillips Exeter class of 1975. We are particularly grateful to Tom because he was our first self-made billionaire interview. We also want to thank Ted White, part of Tom's organization, for his help.

Our partner Mitch Roschelle connected us to Steve Ross, who granted us an interview not only because of Mitch's friendship with Mike Brenner, a member of Steve's executive team, but also because Steve appreciated all the assistance Coopers & Lybrand had provided early in his own career. In addition to Mike, Rosamaria Garibay from Related Companies was enormously helpful.

PwC partner Carol Sawdye, who had just returned to the firm after an extended stint as the executive vice president and CFO of the National Basketball Association, helped us arrange interviews with Micky Arison, Herb Simon, Glen Taylor, and Mark Cuban, all NBA owners. Carol also found the time to participate in these conversations, which was a treat. Linda Danielson at Taylor Corporation, Bonnie

Southers at Simon Property Group, Dawn Knox on Mark Cuban's team, and Jennifer De La Cruz in Micky Arison's office were also big aids in facilitating these interviews.

PwC partner Byron Carlock interested his friend Steve Case in our project. We owe thanks also to Herbie Siskend, Seth London, Marissa Secreto, and Allyson Burns in Case's Revolution organization.

Lou Starita, the cousin of Laura Starita, who is part of John Paul Mitchell Systems, helped us arrange an interview with John Paul DeJoria. Luke Jacobellis and Mayra-Alejandra Garcia in John Paul DeJoria's office were very accommodating as well.

PwC partner Tim O'Hara and managing director Mike Keenan facilitated our interview with Jeff Lurie, the owner of the Philadelphia Eagles. This was a special treat for Mitch Cohen, a Philadelphia native and lifelong Eagles fan. Don Smolenski, Anne Gordon, Tara Sutphen, and Tina D'Orazio in Jeff's office were most helpful.

Mike Keenan also helped us get the interview with the Spanos family—Michael Spanos, Alexis Spanos Ruhl, Dea Spanos Berberian, and Alex Spanos, who helped us understand their dad's journey. We'd also like to thank AG Spanos Companies' Ed McGuire and Natalia Orfanos for their help.

Team member Kate Barnard helped us gain access to T. Boone Pickens by sending him a wonderful animated video she created about our project. Boone was generous with his time and insights. Jay Rosser, BP Capital's vice president of public affairs and Boone's chief of staff, and Monica Long were wonderful hosts during our time in Dallas.

Abby Brennan put the team in touch with Michael Jaharis with the help of Lenny Carr. Jeff Sarrett, Kevin Farro, and Peggy Nicholson, all in the Jaharis companies, facilitated the meeting. Abby and Kate conducted the interview.

Our partner Adam Gutstein connected us to Eric Lefkofsky. Paul Taafe and Pat Garrison on Eric's team also proved instrumental in arranging the interview.

John Bunting, a partner in PwC Canada, helped arrange Chip Wilson's interview, as did Janet Keall on Chip's team. We are also grateful to our PwC Australia colleague Brad Russell and his personal assistant Anne Powell for their help.

Marvin Zonis, an emeritus professor at the University of Chicago Booth School of Business, put us in touch with former student Joe Mansueto. Carling Spelhaug, Nadine Youssef, and Sarabeth Moder on Joe's team made the meeting happen.

Angel Dou and Selina Zhang at PwC China were able to arrange the meeting with Hui Lin Chit. PwC Hong Kong colleague TJ Yen also was most helpful.

PwC Global Chairman Dennis Nally and U.S. Chairman and Senior Partner Bob Moritz supported our work from the beginning and encouraged us every step of the way. Most important, they gave us the time and latitude to work on what was a unique project for us individually and for PwC. PwC Vice Chairman and U.S. Services Leader Dana Mcilwain, U.S. Advisory Operations Leader Mike Koehneman, and U.S. Advisory Leader Miles Everson have been very supportive of the work and have helped us begin implementing some of our findings at PwC.

A number of individuals on the PwC risk management and legal teams played a vital role in the development of this book. Risk management leader Jacqueline Olnyk gave us a green light for the project early on. The following individuals also helped with various issues that arose during the past two years: Paula Adler, Katy Posen, Richard Beaumont, Martin Schmidt, Maulshree Solanki, Diana Weiss, and Iliana Zuniga. Caroline Cheng provided not only legal advice but a very useful, early review. A number of our colleagues read various versions of the book and provided valuable feedback for which we are grateful. They include Joe Duffy, Miles Everson, Greg Garrison, Genevieve Girault, Rob Gittings, Adam Gutstein, Kate Hannah, Becky Harlem, Mike Harvey, Dennis Nally, and Cathrine Vrana. Richard

Edelman, Jen McClellan, and Russ Dubner of Edelman International provided good guidance early on.

A special thank-you goes to our agent, Jacque Murphy, who pitched our book idea to Penguin Portfolio. Adrian Zackheim, CEO of Portfolio, we thank for "getting it" so quickly. We appreciate Emily Angell and Jesse Maeshiro for shepherding us through the process at Portfolio.

We were fortunate to get the assistance of Julia Heskel, a marketing director at PwC. Julia has helped us shepherd the book through finalization, production, and launch.

To spend the past two years working on this while doing our "day jobs" required assistants Adrienne Lozito and Meredith McConnell, who truly organized our professional lives.

Finally, we owe the biggest debt of gratitude to our wives and families. We thank Eileen Sviokla and Carri Cohen for being such patient fans and making it all possible.

We both feel fortunate for the opportunity to study so many creators of great value. It's been a privilege indeed.

APPENDIX
Billionaires Who Appear in This Book

Karl Albrecht
1920–2014, Germany
Aldi Süd (South)

After serving in the army in World War II, Karl Albrecht returned home to Germany and, together with his brother Theodor, took over his mother's corner grocery store. The pair opened successive new stores until 1948, when they incorporated as Aldi Stores Ltd. The company made its name as a provider of affordable goods to a struggling postwar Germany. The brothers eventually split their areas of responsibility, with Karl running Aldi Süd and Theo, Aldi Nord. Aldi Süd had more than 2,500 stores worldwide when Karl Albrecht stepped down from day-to-day operations in 1994.

Theodor Albrecht
1922–2010, Germany
Aldi Nord (North), Trader Joe's

Theo Albrecht was groomed while still a young man to take over his mother's corner grocery store. He and his brother Karl grew the business in the late 1940s and 1950s. A disagreement in 1960 led the brothers to divide up the company's assets. Theodor assumed control of Aldi Nord, which had rights to expand under the Aldi name in the rest of

Europe. In 1979, he bought the California-based Trader Joe's chain of grocery stores. Today, there are approximately 2,500 Aldi Nord stores in Germany, and thousands more throughout continental Europe.

Paul Allen
b. 1953, United States
Microsoft, Vulcan Ventures

Paul Allen was fourteen when he met fellow student and Seattle native Bill Gates. In 1975, the two college dropouts cofounded Microsoft to provide software for the burgeoning personal computer market. Microsoft catapulted to success, and Allen, the chief technologist, became a billionaire. Diagnosed with Hodgkin's disease, he resigned in 1983. After treatment, he founded Vulcan Ventures, an investment firm with large stakes in real estate and technology companies. Today, Allen owns the Portland Trail Blazers of the National Basketball Association and the Seattle Seahawks of the National Football League.

Philip Anschutz
b. 1939, United States
The Anschutz Corporation

Philip Anschutz followed his father and grandfather into oil and gas exploration. Striking oil, he grew his first company into one of the largest oil companies in the United States before diversifying into railroads in the 1980s, when he led the merger of the Southern Pacific and Union Pacific railroads. The following decade, Anschutz expanded into entertainment and telecommunications. He founded Qwest Communications and created the Anschutz Entertainment Group (AEG), which today owns a number of entertainment venues, such as the Staples Center in Los Angeles, as well as various sports teams, such as the LA Kings of the National Hockey League.

Michael Arison
b. 1949, United States
Carnival Cruise Corporation

Micky Arison acquired his taste for the cruise business from his father, who owned various cruising companies when Arison was young. Arison went to work for his father's business when he was a teenager, and gradually acquired more responsibility until Arison senior stepped down. At the time, the Carnival Cruise Lines was a three-ship company, but Arison had a vision of turning cruising into a mainstream vacation option. He purchased smaller companies and invested in more boats. The Carnival parent today owns nearly a dozen cruise lines, including Cunard, Holland America Line, and Princess Cruises. Arison is also the owner of the Miami Heat basketball team.

Steven Ballmer
b. 1956, United States
Microsoft

In 1980, two years after graduating from Harvard, Steve Ballmer was invited by fellow student Bill Gates to join a fledgling Microsoft as its manager of operations. Within a year, Microsoft signed its breakthrough deal with IBM to design an operating system for the company's new product, the personal computer. Ballmer became the marketing and sales guru, and was key to realizing Gates's vision. As second in command, he accumulated significant equity in the company that made him a billionaire. Ballmer became Microsoft's CEO in 2000, when Gates stepped down, and held that position until retiring in 2014. Today, Ballmer is the owner of the Los Angeles Clippers basketball team.

Jeff Bezos

b. 1964, United States

Amazon.com

After graduating from Princeton, Jeff Bezos worked on Wall Street. While at D. E. Shaw & Co., he became the youngest vice president in the investment firm's history. At age twenty-nine, he left to found Internet retailer Amazon.com. The company started off selling books because the international standard book number (ISBN) system made them suitable for Web search and order fulfillment. A wide range of products soon followed. In 2007, Amazon launched the Kindle electronic reader and began selling digital content as well. Today, Amazon.com is the world's largest online retailer. Still CEO, Bezos is also the owner of the *Washington Post.*

Sara Blakely

b. 1971, United States

Spanx

A Florida native, Sara Blakely was working as an office supplies saleswoman by day and a stand-up comic by night when she invented the woman's shapewear product that would later be named Spanx. After years of development, Blakely's big break came in 2000, when her product appeared on the Oprah Winfrey show. The popularity of Spanx skyrocketed, making Blakely a billionaire. Today, the company sells more than two hundred different products, including not only shapewear but also swimwear, jeans, and men's shapewear. Blakely continues to be Spanx's spokesperson and leading product innovator.

Michael Bloomberg

b. 1942, United States

Bloomberg, LP

After graduating from Johns Hopkins University and Harvard Business School, Michael Bloomberg took a job with Salomon Brothers.

He rose through the ranks to become a general partner in 1972, but was let go when Salomon Brothers was acquired in 1981. Bloomberg received a $10 million severance package and used that money to start what would become Bloomberg LP, a financial data publishing company. Bloomberg also publishes *Bloomberg Businessweek*. Michael Bloomberg left business full-time to serve as the mayor of New York City from 2002–14. Today he is actively involved in philanthropic issues to do with the environment and health, and he is the UN secretary general's special envoy for cities and climate change.

Sir Richard Branson
b. 1950, United Kingdom
Virgin Group, Ltd.

In 1970, Richard Branson launched his first company, a mail-order record business, which he shortly supplemented with a music label and retail store. His label signed iconic, controversial bands like the Sex Pistols, and his retail stores morphed into the Virgin Megastores. Branson also started expanding into areas beyond music, including the airline industry with the launch of Virgin Atlantic Airways in the early 1980s, trains (Virgin Trains) and telecommunications (Virgin Mobile) in the 1990s, and space tourism (Virgin Galactic) in 2004. Today, the Virgin Group consists of four hundred companies. Branson remains as chairman, while pursuing philanthropic efforts to combat global warming.

Sergey Brin
b. 1973, Russia
Google, Inc.

Born in Moscow, Sergey Brin immigrated to the United States with his parents at the age of six. As a PhD student at Stanford, he met fellow student Larry Page, and together the two embarked on research to find a better way to conduct Web searches. Their findings eventually led to the development of the Google search engine, and the launching of the eponymous company in 1998. Brin served as the president of technology at Google from 2001 to 2011. He continues today as assistant secretary of Google, and shares responsibility for running the company with Page and Eric Schmidt.

Eli Broad
b. 1933, United States
KB Home, SunAmerica

At age twenty, Eli Broad set up an accounting business in an unused office of Donald Kaufman's home-building business in Detroit. In 1957, the two men founded Kaufman & Broad (now known as KB Home) to build starter homes. Because the houses lacked basements, they were much less expensive to build, and more affordable to people flocking to the suburbs during the postwar baby boom. During the early 1960s, the company expanded into the Southwest. Broad moved beyond home building and purchased the Sun Life Insurance company in 1971, transforming it into financial investment firm SunAmerica. AIG purchased SunAmerica in 1999; Broad stepped down as CEO the following year to focus on the Eli and Edythe Broad Foundation.

Warren Buffett
b. 1930, United States
Berkshire Hathaway

Commonly referred to as the most successful investor of his generation, Warren Buffet started his business career as a child, making his first investment at the age of eleven and his first entrepreneurial venture at thirteen. After graduating from business school, he established investing partnerships and developed his lifelong practice of investing only in undervalued companies. This approach allowed Buffett to acquire control in 1962 over Berkshire Hathaway, a textile company he transformed first into a holding company for insurance businesses, and later into a large conglomerate, with investments in

GEICO, Dairy Queen, HJ Heinz, and others. Buffett continues to be CEO of Berkshire Hathaway and is an active philanthropist.

Yan Cheung
b. 1957, China
Nine Dragons Paper Ltd., America Chung Nam

Born in a coal-mining district in northeast China, Cheung began working while still a teenager. In her late twenties, she started her first business, a paper pulp company in Hong Kong. Despite its success, in 1990 she moved to California, where recycled paper products were more abundant. America Chung Nam, her recycled pulp manufacturer, became the country's largest paper exporter by 2001. Cheung started a counterpart company in China in 1996, Nine Dragons Paper, which buys pulp from America Chung Nam and others and uses it to create paper packaging. Cheung remains the chairwoman of Nine Dragons Paper.

Mark Cuban
b. 1958, United States
Broadcast.com, Dallas Mavericks, Magnolia Pictures, Landmark Theaters

While in college, serial entrepreneur Mark Cuban started various ventures to make money, including running a pub and giving disco dancing lessons. Soon after graduating, he launched MicroSolutions, which he and partner Martin Woodall sold to CompuServ in 1990 for $6 million. From then on, Cuban acted as a private investor for ideas he believed had high potential. One was a nascent Web-based broadcast technology that became the basis for Broadcast.com. Cuban and partner Todd Wagner sold Broadcast.com to Yahoo in 1999 for more than $5 billion in Yahoo stock. Today, Cuban owns the Dallas Mavericks basketball franchise, film distributor Magnolia Pictures, and the Landmark Theaters chain.

John Paul DeJoria

b. 1944, United States
John Paul Mitchell Systems, Patrón Spirits

John Paul DeJoria grew up in Los Angeles in modest circumstances. While a salesman in the haircare industry for Redken and the Institute of Trichology, he attended a hair conference, where he met celebrity stylist Paul Mitchell. The two launched haircare company John Paul Mitchell Systems in 1980 with the strategy of selling exclusively to salons. In addition to selling the products, DeJoria trained salon owners on how to sell to consumers. In 1989, he cofounded Patrón Spirits with Martin Crowley. DeJoria is also an executive producer and actor.

Michael Dell

b. 1965, United States
Dell Computer

Michael Dell started building computer upgrade kits in his University of Texas at Austin dorm room as a freshman, selling directly to customers with great success. A year later, Dell Computer Corporation was incorporated, and its first proprietary computers soon followed. During the Internet boom, Dell grew rapidly on account of its direct-to-customer sales model as well as its extremely efficient supply chain. Michael Dell stepped down as CEO in 2004, but returned as a result of a decline in the PC market, quality issues, and SEC charges. In 2013, he organized a successful leveraged buyout to bring the company private.

Sir James Dyson

b. 1947, United Kingdom
Dyson

James Dyson was a student at the Royal College of Art in London when Rotork Marine granted his first design commission for a flat-hulled boat. Dyson, however, is best known for his eponymous bagless vacuum cleaners. The first model, the G-Force, went through

5,127 iterations before it was ready for production in the mid-1980s; however, Dyson had difficulty finding a manufacturer in the United Kingdom or the United States. In 1993, he launched his own manufacturing company, which he continues to head today. He is also the founder of the James Dyson Foundation, whose mission is to encourage creativity in young people.

Phillip Frost
b. circa 1935, United States
Key Pharmaceuticals, Ivax Corporation, Teva Pharmaceutical
Industries, Protalix BioTherapeutics

Phillip Frost was a dermatology professor at the University of Miami when he and Michael Jaharis took over Key Pharmaceuticals in 1972. After they sold the company to Schering-Plough in 1986, Frost served as chairman and CEO of generic drug maker Ivax. Teva Pharmaceuticals acquired Ivax for $7.4 billion in 2006, and he eventually became chairman of the board. Frost has been the CEO and chairman of OPKO Health since 2007. He is a generous benefactor of the University of Miami School of Music, the Miami Art Museum, and the Miami Museum of Science, all of which have been renamed after him and his wife, Patricia.

Bill Gates
b. 1955, United States
Microsoft Corporation

Bill Gates was twenty years old when he founded Microsoft Corporation with partner Paul Allen in 1976—famously choosing to pursue entrepreneurship instead of completing his degree at Harvard. With the first commercially available operating system for IBM-compatible personal computers, Gates established Microsoft as a major player in the software market. Microsoft became known not only for the Windows operating system but also for its consumer electronics and computers. In 2000, the American tech billionaire established the Bill & Melinda Gates Foundation. Gate stepped down as CEO of Microsoft in 2008 to dedicate himself to the foundation.

Terry Gou
b. 1950, Taiwan
Foxconn (Hon Hai Precision, Ltd.)

Terry Gou has spent his entire career manufacturing name-brand products on behalf of the companies that sell them. His first company produced the knobs used on televisions to change channels. By the early 1980s, Gou's company was manufacturing personal computer accessories, including joysticks for Atari. By 1988 the Taiwan plant lacked sufficient capacity, so Gou built a factory in Shenzhen. That expansion allowed him to become a supplier to Compaq and other computer companies. Today, Hon Hai, China's largest exporter, manufactures a number of popular consumer electronics, including the Amazon Kindle, the Apple iPad, and the Nintendo Wii.

Hui Lin Chit
b. 1954, China
Hengan International Group

Born in Fujian province, Hui Lin Chit was working as a farmer when he started his first business, a zipper company. He had begun manufacturing simple clothing when he met Sze Man Bok, another businessman, and with him founded Hengan International to make sanitary products for lower-income women. Hengan made both men billionaires. The company became listed on the Hong Kong Stock Exchange in 1998. Today, Hengan is one of the largest domestic producers of sanitary napkins, baby diapers, and napkins in China. Hui Lin Chit continues to be CEO. He is also the deputy chairman of Fujian Province Industry and Trade Association and the chairman of Guangzhou City Trade Association.

Mohammed Ibrahim

b. 1946, Sudan

Celtel

Sudanese by birth, Mo Ibrahim moved to the UK to earn advanced degrees in engineering and telecommunications. He spent his early professional life with British Telecom, which he left in 1989 to start the telecommunication consultancy MSI. In 2000, Ibrahim sold MSI to concentrate on Celtel, a venture to provide mobile telecommunications services in Africa. Acquiring telecommunications licenses for a number of African countries, Celtel became one of the first telecommunications firms to deliver service to Africans at the "bottom of the pyramid." Ibrahim sold Celtel in 2005, and now focuses on the Mo Ibrahim Foundation to improve governance in Africa.

Marian Ilitch

b. 1933, United States

Little Caesars Pizza; Ilitch Holdings, Inc.; Detroit Tigers and Detroit Red Wings; MotorCity Casino

Marian Ilitch started out in the food business as a young girl, helping out in her father's restaurant. She was a Delta Airlines clerk when she met Michael. After she gave birth to their third child (of seven), they opened the first Little Caesars Restaurant; Michael baked the pizzas and Marian managed the finances. One of the first restaurants that only sold in a carry-out model, Little Caesars had fewer costs and lower prices than competitors, and so grew rapidly. In 1992, annual sales of the private company exceeded $2.1 billion. In 1996, the Ilitches created Olympia Development to focus on building projects in downtown Detroit.

Michael Ilitch

b. 1929, United States
Little Caesars Pizza; Ilitch Holdings, Inc.; Detroit Tigers and Detroit Red Wings;
MotorCity Casino

Michael Ilitch began his career playing baseball in the Detroit Tigers farm league. He then held various jobs, including one at a restaurant/bar where he learned to throw pizza. Ilitch opened the first Little Caesars restaurant with his wife, Marian, in 1959; franchising soon followed. The business flourished in the 1970s as the number of American working women increased, as did the need for inexpensive meal options. The 1990s "Pizza Pizza" marketing campaign, Michael's brainchild, caused a boom in business with its promise to feed a family of four for less than $10. Ilitch bought the Detroit Red Wings hockey team and the Detroit Tigers baseball team in 1992.

Michael Jaharis

b. 1928, United States
Key Pharmaceuticals, Vatera Healthcare Partners, Arisaph Pharmaceuticals

Michael Jaharis earned his law degree and went to work for Miles Laboratories, the makers of Alka-Seltzer, where he rose to become the lead counsel. He left in 1972 to acquire Key Pharmaceuticals with fellow billionaire Phillip Frost. While at Key, Jaharis worked to improve upon or adjust the delivery system of a number of the company's main products. This approach resulted in the creation of top-selling asthma and hypertension products. Jaharis and Frost sold Key in 1986 to Schering-Plough, and Jaharis went on to found Kos Pharmaceuticals, which marketed the first niacin product that is well tolerated and effective at increasing good cholesterol. Jaharis sold Kos to Abbot Laboratories. He has since founded Vatera Healthcare Partners, a health venture capital firm, and Arisaph Pharmaceuticals, a biotech discovery firm.

Steve Jobs
1955–2011, United States
Apple Computer, Pixar

Jobs was a game designer at Atari when he, Steve Wozniak, and Ronald Wayne launched Apple Computer in 1976 to market a personal computer Wozniak had invented. The first Apple PCs proved a huge success, but later products floundered. Infighting led to Jobs's 1985 ouster. He founded NeXT Computer and bought the Pixar animation studio from George Lucas. Pixar's 1995 IPO made Jobs a billionaire. Two years later, Apple bought NeXT and reinstated Jobs as CEO, ushering in an era of tremendous innovation and growth driven by the iPod, iPhone, and iPad. Steve Jobs died of pancreatic cancer in 2011.

Kirk Kerkorian
b. 1917, United States
International Leisure, MGM/United Artists, MGM Resorts International

A flight instructor as a young man, Kirk Kerkorian then risked his life flying mosquito bombers for the Canadian Royal Air Force during World War II. In 1947, he purchased charter flight company Trans International Airlines. He sold the airline for $104 million in 1968. Kerkorian went on to acquire movie studio Metro Goldwyn Mayer and built numerous Las Vegas hotels and casinos. Later a powerful force in the auto industry, he made two unsuccessful takeover bids for Chrysler and purchased large amounts of General Motors and Ford stock. He stepped down from the MGM Resorts International board in 2011. Now ninety-six, Kerkorian is still active in business.

Eric Lefkofsky
b. 1969, United States
Groupon

Eric Lefkofsky founded multiple companies with his partner, Brad Keywell, before launching Lightbank, a venture capital firm that invests in technology start-ups whose products deliver social and mobile services. Groupon, which offers vouchers for a wide range of goods and services in cities around the world, is the best-known company in the Lightbank portfolio companies, and the one that made Lefkofsky a billionaire. Groupon went public in 2011. Two years later, Lefkofsky became CEO and is still in that role today.

Ming Chung Liu

b. 1962, Taiwan

Nine Dragons Paper Ltd.; America Chung Nam

A Brazilian citizen of Chinese descent, Ming Chung Liu went to the United States as a young man to train to be a dentist. In the late 1980s he met Yan Cheung, a young entrepreneur who had launched paper pulp company in Hong Kong. Since Hong Kong had only limited paper resources, in 1990 the couple moved to California to start America Chung Nam to leverage the abundance of recycled materials in the United States. They then established paper manufacturer Nine Dragons Paper, Ltd., in China. As the current CEO of Nine Dragons, Ming Chung Liu is responsible for business operations and management.

Che Woo Lui

b. 1929, Hong Kong

K. Wah Group, Galaxy Entertainment Group

Dr. Lui was just fourteen in 1940s Hong Kong when he started his first business: a wholesale food company. His next venture sold wholesale automotive parts. After that he resold construction and quarrying equipment left over in Korea by the U.S. military at the end of the Korean War and then got into quarrying construction supplies from the mountains edging Hong Kong. He eventually got into the construction business himself and established K. Wah International Holdings, best known as a hotel developer in Hong Kong—Woo negotiated one of the first Hong Kong hotel deals with a Western hotel chain, Holiday Inn. More recently, Woo founded Galaxy Entertainment Group, developer of one of the most successful gambling resorts in Macau.

Jeffrey Lurie
b. 1951, United States
Philadelphia Eagles

Jeffrey Lurie, a PhD in social policy, left his position as a college professor to work for General Cinema, a movie theater chain founded by his grandfather. After a few years, Lurie launched the production company Harcourt; one of his films, *Inside Job,* won an Academy Award. In 1994 Lurie acquired the Philadelphia Eagles football team for $185 million, at the time the highest amount ever paid for an NFL franchise. Making significant early investments in the Eagles' infrastructure, Lurie revitalized the franchise. Lurie continues to own and run the Eagles today.

Jack Ma
b. 1964, China
Alibaba.com

Jack Ma taught himself to speak English as a young man by giving tours to visiting English-speaking businessmen. Ma launched online directory China Pages with $2,000 he borrowed; the company, which failed, was reportedly China's first Internet company. In 1999, Ma launched Alibaba.com with seventeen others; his goal was to help Chinese companies connect with the world. Alibaba is now a collection of businesses that compose China's largest e-commerce enterprise. Alibaba Group is preparing for an IPO.

Joe Mansueto

b. 1956, United States

Morningstar

A graduate of the University of Chicago Booth School of Business, Joe Mansueto was a serial entrepreneur and investing hobbyist who worked for a number of financial services companies before launching Morningstar in 1984. What began as a quarterly publication describing and evaluating four hundred mutual funds grew into an enterprise that provides objective commentary and analysis to individual investors, institutional investors, and financial advisers worldwide. The company, which went public in 2005, currently provides data on approximately 473,000 investment offerings. Mansueto remains the CEO of Morningstar; he is also the owner of *Inc.* and *Fast Company* magazines.

Dietrich Mateschitz

b. 1944, Austria

Red Bull, GmbH

The Austrian billionaire began his career as a marketing executive, first with Unilever and later with the German consumer goods company Blendax. Mateschitz, together with Thai businessmen Chaleo and Chalerm Yoovidhya, cofounded Red Bull in 1987 to market the sweet energy drinks he had encountered during business trips in Asia. Reformulating the drinks to appeal to a Western palette, Mateschitz launched them first in Austria, then expanded into other markets. Red Bull grew quickly due to its international advertising strategy of associating the drink with extreme sports; Matechitz has solidified this connection by sponsoring extreme athletes and buying racing teams, among others. Though reclusive, Mateschitz is still actively involved in his company's expansion.

Sunil Mittal

b. 1957, India
Bharti Enterprises, Ltd.

After college, Sunil Mittal started various business ventures, selling bicycle crankshafts and importing Suzuki portable generators. He then got into the telecommunications industry, first importing and then manufacturing telephone handsets for brands like Siemens and LG. In 1994, Mittal partnered with British Telecom and Telecom Italia to offer mobile and Internet service. Bharti Airtel went public in 2002, making Mittal a billionaire. As chairman and CEO of Bharti Enterprises, Mittal continues to lead the company's expansion in the telecommunications space as well as in retail, financial services, and manufacturing.

Rupert Murdoch

b. 1931, Australia
News Corporation

The international media magnate inherited his first business at the age of twenty-two when his father, an Australian journalist and newspaper publisher, died. Murdoch grew those businesses for fifteen years, amassing an estimated $50 million fortune, before he started acquiring London-based newspapers and tabloids, then American newspapers in the late 1960s. In 1985, he branched into film and television by purchasing 20th Century Fox and creating the Fox Broadcasting Company. Other acquisitions include HarperCollins and the *Wall Street Journal*. Today, Murdoch remains executive chairman of News Corporation, while continuing to make headlines for his efforts to acquire more media properties.

Elon Musk
b. 1971, South Africa
Tesla, PayPal

The South African native and serial entrepreneur founded multiple businesses before the ones that made him famous. In 1999, he co-founded X.com, an online financial services and e-mail company. A year later X-com merged with Cofinity, along with its online bank subsidiary, PayPal. Under Musk's leadership, PayPal grew dramatically until it was sold to eBay in 2002 for $1.5 billion in stock. He then invested in the company that would become Tesla, a manufacturer of electronic vehicles. Musk is also the founder of SpaceX, an aerospace company pursuing innovations to pave the way for space tourism, as well as for exploration and colonization of Mars.

Pierre Omidyar
b. 1967, France
eBay, Omidyar Network

Born in France, Pierre Omidyar moved to the United States as a child. He attended Tufts University in Boston, and worked for Claris, a subsidiary of Apple, before starting Ink Development Corporation, a retail business that also engaged in Internet sales. The company was bought by Apple in 1996 under the name eShop. Omidyar had by then already launched eBay as an auction service built into his personal Web site. The service grew exponentially. By 1998, eBay's annual revenue exceeded $45 million. That same year, the company went public, and Omidyar became a billionaire. He now dedicates his time to the Omidyar Network, a philanthropic investment bank.

Larry Page

b. 1973, United States

Google

Google grew out of a Stanford graduate school project that Larry Page and Sergey Brin conducted to identify a better way to do Web searches. Their invention, which they called Google, made it easier to find information on the Web, and served as the basis of the 1998 launch of the company. Since then, Google has evolved into an Internet behemoth known for content search, Web ad displays, video streaming (through YouTube), productivity applications, cloud storage, maps, driverless cars, and mobile devices. Page has served as Google's CEO since 2011.

Lynda Resnick

b. 1944, United States

Roll International (Fiji Water, POM Wonderful, Wonderful Pistachios, Teleflora)

Lynda Resnick started her own ad agency in Los Angeles when she was only nineteen years old. She met Stuart Resnick, her second husband, in 1969, and ten years later the two acquired Teleflora, the flower delivery service. Throughout the 70s and 80s the couple expanded their holdings to include citrus groves, pistachios, and other tree farms, and Lynda applied her marketing acumen to develop and position her products. She is responsible for making the pomegranate a familiar fruit in the United States, for the "get cracking" advertising campaign for Wonderful Pistachios, and for the success of FIJI water.

Stephen Ross

b. 1940, United States

Related Companies

Stephen Ross founded the Related Companies in 1972 after leaving his job at Bear Stearns. From the outset, Ross wanted to build a diversified real estate business involved in leasing, development, and syndication of commercial and retail properties. Some of Ross's best-known projects to date include the Time Warner Center in New York City, and the current Hudson Yards Project under way on the far West Side of Manhattan. Stephen Ross also owns the Miami Dolphins football team, as well as the Sun Life Stadium in which the team plays.

Sheryl Sandberg
b. 1969, United States
Facebook

After earning her undergraduate and business school degrees at Harvard University, Sheryl Sandberg worked for Larry Summers at the World Bank, and then at the Treasury Department, where she was his chief of staff. When the Democratic Party lost the 2000 election, Sandberg moved to Silicon Valley to get in on the Internet boom. Recruited by Google, she rose through the ranks rapidly; Sandberg is credited with managing the ad deals that made the company profitable. In 2007 she was approached by Mark Zuckerberg, the founder of Facebook, who was looking for an experienced business partner to help him run the social media giant. Sandberg joined the company as its COO, a role she holds today.

Eric Schmidt
b. 1955, United States
Google, Inc.

When Eric Schmidt became CEO of Google in 2001, he had already spent close to twenty years as an executive at technology companies like Sun Microsystems and Novell. Reportedly Schmidt was brought in to Google to offer a business-minded balance to the technological creativity of founders Sergey Brin and Larry Page. More than a decade later, Schmidt is acknowledged for building strong external relationships for Google with investors, business partners, government agencies, and others. He currently serves as the executive chairman of the company.

Howard Schultz
b. 1953, United States
Starbucks Coffee Company

Howard Schultz was selling kitchen equipment and housewares for a Swedish company when he first encountered Starbucks Coffee Company, a small chain of coffee roasters. In 1981, he joined Starbucks as its director of marketing. After experiencing the espresso bar in Italy, he proposed that Starbucks offer espresso beverages, but his idea was rejected. He left Starbucks to open his own café in 1986, returning shortly after to purchase the chain and turn it into a network of coffeehouses known for its high-quality coffee and espresso. Today, there are 5,500 Starbucks locations worldwide. After a hiatus, Schultz resumed his role as CEO in 2008, a position he still holds today.

Thomas Secunda
b. 1954, United States
Bloomberg

Tom Secunda had worked with Michael Bloomberg at Salomon Brothers. In 1982 they joined forces to start Bloomberg LP., a business that provides financial data and analysis via proprietary terminals to financial traders. A technical whiz, Secunda designed and developed working products in keeping with Michael Bloomberg's vision. He served as the company's chief information officer for many years, a role in which he oversaw research and development of new products. Today, Secunda is the firm's vice chairman.

Herbert Simon

b. 1934, United States

Simon Property Group, Indiana Pacers

A Brooklyn, New York, native, Herbert Simon moved to Indianapolis at the age of twenty-two. He and his brother Melvin worked for a real estate broker for a few years, after which they started their own business leasing and developing retail properties. Things took off when the Montgomery Ward department store leased a location in one of their malls; that relationship opened opportunities with other major retailers, such as JCPenney. Today, the Simon Property Group is one of the largest developers of shopping malls in the United States. In 1983, Herbert and Melvin purchased the Indiana Pacers basketball team, which Herbert still owns.

Melvin Simon

1926–2009, United States

Simon Property Group

Melvin Simon was a young man when he settled in Indianapolis and went to work for a real estate broker selling leases for commercial properties. He persuaded his brothers Herbert and Frank to join him there. After a few years, the brothers launched Melvin Simon and Associates, a real estate leasing and development firm. Melvin's extreme charisma and salesmanship brought about early success for the company. As it grew, Melvin and Herbert shared responsibilities, and the company morphed into the Simon Property Group, one of the largest developers of shopping malls in the United States.

Alexander Spanos

b. 1923, United States

AG Spanos Companies, San Diego Chargers

Alex Spanos worked for his father in the family bakery in Stockton, California, until the age of twenty-seven. Borrowing $800, he launched a roadside sandwich truck to feed migrant workers who came to the Stockton area to work on the local farms during the growing and picking seasons. The venture mushroomed into a large catering and housing business. A few years later, he started buying buildings, then moved on to develop his own properties. The AG Spanos Companies today is one of the largest developers of multifamily residential buildings in the United States. Spanos owns 97 percent of the San Diego Chargers football team.

Thomas Steyer
b. 1957, United States
Farallon Capital

Tom Steyer worked for Morgan Stanley and for Goldman Sachs before launching the hedge fund Farallon Capital Management in 1986. Steyer was reportedly the first hedge fund manager to court university endowments as investors. Yale University, his undergraduate alma mater, was one of the first universities to sign on. Steyer's fund far outperformed the market over the course of twenty years of investing, leading to dramatic growth in the endowments and individual fortunes that were invested in Farallon. A well-known environmentalist, Steyer sold his stake in Farallon in 2012, and has dedicated himself to environmental issues and supporting progressive political candidates.

Glen Taylor
b. 1941, United States
Taylor Corporation

While still a college student, Glen Taylor got a job with Carlson Letter Service, a local printing shop in Minnesota. Upon graduation, Taylor grew the mom-and-pop proprietor into a large regional provider by focusing on wedding stationery and related accessories. After buying out his boss and two other business partners, he renamed the business the Taylor Corporation and turned it into one of the largest custom printing and electronic companies in the United States. Today,

Taylor still runs the privately held company. He is also the owner of the Minnesota Timberwolves basketball team.

Chip Wilson
b. 1956, Canada
Westbeach Snowboard Ltd., Lululemon
Chip Wilson grew up in Vancouver, Canada, and went to work on the Alaska pipeline while still a teen. He reportedly earned enough money to put himself through college and launch his first company, Westbeach Snowboard Ltd., which made surf, skate, and snowboarding apparel designed by Wilson to meet his own tastes. Wilson led Westbeach from 1979–95, and sold the company in 1997 due to declining sales. In 1998, Wilson launched Lululemon Athletica to take advantage of the growing interest in yoga. Until 2005, Wilson's role at the yoga apparel retailer focused on design and creative, though he remained chairman of the board until 2013, when he stepped down. He retains a board seat.

Oprah Winfrey
b. 1954, United States
The *Oprah Winfrey Show,* Oprah Winfrey Network, O: *The Oprah Magazine*
Mississippian Oprah Winfrey began her media career in high school with a job in radio. She quickly moved on to daytime TV and hosted a talk show, *AM Chicago,* which in 1986 became the *Oprah Winfrey Show.* Oprah formed a production company and syndicated the popular show. Oprah's weekday program ran for twenty-five years, and is now viewed in more than one hundred countries. She went on to cofound Oxygen Media and the Oprah Winfrey Network. Winfrey has had a vibrant acting career that includes an Academy Award nomination. She has also produced numerous films and TV series. Oprah Winfrey uses her celebrity to promote philanthropic work for educational causes.

Steve Wynn

b. 1942, United States

Wynn Resorts, Ltd.

Steve Wynn's father died when he was a young man, leaving him a chain of bingo parlors in Maryland. Wynn took over and ran the parlors, and used his profits to invest in a hotel and casino in Las Vegas. Wynn's profits allowed him to buy and sell more land, while renovating and expanding other investment properties. Purchasing the Las Vegas locale the Golden Nugget, he revamped it into a full casino and resort and featured headline acts such as Frank Sinatra. Today, Wynn's multiple properties on the Las Vegas strip also include the Bellagio and the Mirage; he also owns the Golden Nugget in Atlantic City, and the Wynn Macau casino and resort, reportedly the first Vegas-style resort there.

Tadashi Yanai

b. 1949, Japan

Fast Retailing (Uniqlo)

Tadashi Yanai took over his father's small men's clothing business in 1984 and a year later opened the first Unique Clothing Warehouse (shortened to Uniqlo) in Hiroshima. A subsidiary of Fast Retailing, Uniqlo focused on stocking affordable, classic casual pieces. The idea took off, and within ten years there were one hundred Uniqlo stores in Japan. In 2000, a fleece sweatshirt offered in many different colors made Uniqlo a household name and set the stage for further expansion in Japan and around the world. Today, the company continues to grow its Uniqlo brand in international markets, with stores in New York and London.

Mark Zuckerberg

b. 1984, United States

Facebook

Mark Zuckerberg matriculated at Harvard University in 2002 and quickly built his reputation as one of the best computer programmers on campus. This caught the attention of a trio of students who were developing a match-making program. Zuckerberg joined the project, but soon left to team up with friends Dustin Moskovitz, Chris Hughes, and Eduardo Saverin to develop the social network that would become Facebook. Zuckerberg left Harvard at the end of his second year to dedicate himself to Facebook full-time. He moved Facebook's headquarters to Palo Alto, California, and took in outside investment to grow the business. Today, Facebook has more than one billion users worldwide. Zuckerberg is still the CEO and chairman of the board, and is active in philanthropic activities, particularly in the field of education.

NOTES

___

Introduction

1. For more details on PwC's 2014 CEO survey, to watch videos of CEOs sharing their ideas for the future, or to download the full report, see http://www.pwc.com/us/en/ceo-survey-us/index.jhtml, accessed February 14, 2014.

2. In subsequent years, the number of self-made billionaires noted in the 2013 and 2014 *Forbes* list rose significantly. We attribute this increase to increased health in economic markets all around the world. The increases, in short, are market driven, not structural, and they support our findings.

3. Neuroscience research has a long way to go to explain the actual mechanisms operating in the brain when people are imagining new systems versus judging what is actual. Nonetheless, different patterns of thought and sometimes different regions of the brain seem to be associated with exercising imagination and judgment. And the more you exercise one of these skills, the harder it is to excel at the other.

Chapter 1: Exploding Myths of Extreme Entrepreneurship

1. Duff McDonald, "Red Bull's Billionaire Maniac," *Bloomberg Businessweek,* May 19, 2011.

2. For more on Dietrich Mateschitz and the story of Red Bull, see ibid.; Bryan Curtis, "Herr Mateschitz Wants to Juice You Up," *New York Times Magazine,* October 29, 2006; and Sholto Byrnes, "Flying High on Red Bull Individual Philosophy Underpins Marketing Triumph," *Sunday Tribune* (Ireland), September 1, 2005.

3. One of the sources of contradiction is the fact that there isn't a commonly shared definition of entrepreneur, much less "successful entrepreneur." Some studies include anyone who started a business, skewed toward small businesses. Others only look at those whose companies grew rapidly right from the beginning. Some focus on specific industries; some focus on just the first year, others on ten years or more.

4. Note that we did this analysis on a country level, not an individual billionaire level. The removal of a billionaire from our sample should not be interpreted to mean that we looked into this person specifically and found him or her to be corrupt, but rather that we questioned whether the competitive environment where he or she operated was fair, and so we eliminated all self-made billionaires based in that country so that our sample truly included only those whose wealth came through independent action and acumen.

5. Rotman School of Management Dean Roger Martin coined the concept of "integrative thinking" in his book *The Opposable Mind* (Cambridge, MA: Harvard Business School Press, 2007). Martin argues that successful business leaders are able to hold two opposing ideas in their minds at once, synthesize them, and come up with a novel alternative. While our research complements Martin's work, the dualities we identified from our work with self-made billionaires are not, in all cases, built from strictly opposing forces. Nor in practice do our dualities manifest just as integrative thinking. It is important to

note that billionaires take their dual habits of mind to practice integrative *doing,* meaning that they keep together functions or practices that other organizations might disaggregate.

6. Amanda Fortini, "Pomegranate Princess," *New Yorker,* March 31, 2008, 92–99.

Chapter 2: Empathetic Imagination

1. Unless otherwise noted, all details and quotes to do with Joe Mansueto come from an in-person interview conducted by the authors on November 20, 2012.

2. Neuroscientists are still discovering the exact neurological mechanisms associated with creative thought. Indeed, the mechanisms, portions of the brain involved, and other factors seem to vary depending on the task and the expected output. The study that captured and theorized that creative people are able to hold dual modes of thought was led by neuroscientist Kalina Christoff. In it, she writes, "What creative individuals may share in common is a heightened ability to engage in contradictory modes of thought, including cognitive and affective, and deliberate and spontaneous processing. Although questions remain, the findings provide a valuable starting point for future studies that can provide an even more detailed account of how the brain supports creative thinking and the types of processes that facilitate it." Published in *NeuroImage* 59 (2012): 1783–94.

3. Unless otherwise noted, all details and direct quotes from Jeffrey Lurie come from an in-person interview conducted with the authors on May 30, 2013.

4. John Helyar, "Hail and Farewell: NFL Story: New Man Takes Over the Eagles That Laid Golden Eggs—Owner Braman Grew

Sadder but Richer; Will Lurie Tread the Same Path?—The American Boy's Dream," *Wall Street Journal,* August 18, 1994.

5.   Unless otherwise noted, all direct quotes from Chip Wilson come from an interview conducted with the authors on March 11, 2013.

6.   The Big Five personality traits identified in the psychology literature refer to dimensions of human personality. The Big Five traits are openness to experience, conscientiousness, extroversion, agreeableness, and neuroticism. People are evaluated based on how much of a certain trait they exhibit.

7.   Eli Broad, *The Art of Being Unreasonable: Lessons in Unconventional Thinking* (New York: Wiley, 2012).

8.   For more details on Mateschitz and Red Bull, see Duff McDonald, "Red Bull's Billionaire Maniac," *Bloomberg Businessweek,* May 19, 2011.

9.   Unless otherwise noted, all details and quotes to do with Mark Cuban come from an in-person interview conducted by the authors on July 22, 2013.

10.   Mark Cuban, *How to Win at the Sport of Business: If I Can Do It, You Can Do It* (Self-published e-book, 2011).

11.   Unless otherwise noted, all details and quotes to do with Steve Case come from an in-person interview conducted by the authors on June 19, 2013.

12.   We refer to each billionaire according to the conventions of address that dominate in that person's country. In the United States, Canada, and Europe, standard practice dictates that once we introduce the billionaire by his entire name, it is acceptable to continue using just the last name. In Asia, in contrast, standard practice is to refer to

a person as Mr. or Mrs., or by a chosen title. Given that convention, Mr. Chit is Mr. Chit, whereas someone like Chip Wilson is Wilson.

13. For details, see Blakely's interview with CNN's Fareed Zakaria, in which she discusses her early rejections and ultimate deal making with the hosiery manufacturer, at http://globalpublicsquare.blogs.cnn .com/2013/08/24/sara-blakely-spanx-and-the-american-dream/, accessed January 27, 2014.

14. C. K. Prahalad and Gary Hamel, "Core Competence of the Corporation," *Harvard Business Review* (Fall 1990).

15. Unless otherwise noted, all details and quotes to do with Glen Taylor come from an in-person interview conducted by the authors on February 20, 2013.

16. *Undercover Boss* is a reality-TV franchise in which owners or senior executives of established businesses go undercover as employees to learn about how the work gets done in the organization.

17. Adrian J. Slywotzky, *Value Migration: How to Think Several Moves Ahead of the Competition* (Cambridge, MA: Harvard Business Review Press, 1995).

Chapter 3: Patient Urgency

1. Unless otherwise noted, all details and quotes from Eric Lefkofsky come from an in-person interview between the billionaire and the authors, conducted in the Lightbank offices in Chicago, on December 10, 2012.

2. Sunil Mittal talks about the early years of his business and how he grew Airtel in "Bharti Group's Sunil Bharti Mittal on Lessons of Entrepreneurship and Leadership," *India Knowledge@Wharton*, July 10, 2008.

3. CNN—*Talk Asia*, March 3, 2012.

4.   Ibid.

5.   Unless otherwise noted, the details of Steve Case's story and all quotes come from an in-person interview between the billionaire and the authors, conducted in the Revolution offices in Washington, D.C., on June 19, 2013.

6.   Unless otherwise noted, the details of Alex Spanos's story and all quotes come from an in-person interview between the authors and the billionaire's four children on March 25, 2013.

7.   Alex Spanos writes about his experience and thoughts at the time in his autobiography *Sharing the Wealth: My Story* (Washington, D.C.: Regnery Publishing, 2002).

8.   For more on Rex Jung and his research on *transient hypofrontality*, listen to an interview between him and Krista Tippett, host of the NPR radio show *On Being:* "Rex Jung on Creativity and the Everyday Brain," http://www.onbeing.org/program/creativity-and-everyday-brain/1879, accessed January 20, 2014.

9.   Teresa M. Amabile, Jennifer S. Mueller, William B. Simpson, Constance N. Hadley, Steven J. Kramer, and Lee Flemming, "Time Pressure and Creativity in Organizations," Harvard Business School working paper.

10.   Walter Isaacson, *Steve Jobs* (New York: Simon & Schuster, 2011).

Chapter 4: Inventive Execution

1.   Unless otherwise noted, all details and quotes about Michael Jaharis come from an in-person interview conducted with the authors on June 27, 2013.

2.   Dana Mattioli, "Lululemon's Secret Sauce," *Wall Street Journal* online, updated March 22, 2012.

3. Eli Broad, *The Art of Being Unreasonable: Lessons in Unconventional Thinking* (New York: Wiley, 2012).

4. Ken Auletta, "The Dictator Index: A Billionaire Battles a Continent's Legacy of Misrule," *New Yorker,* May 7, 2011.

5. The Wharton School business professor George Day together with Fuqua School of Business professor Christine Moorman discuss the common corporate tendency of inside-out thinking in their recent book *Strategy from the Outside In: Profiting from Customer Value* (New York: McGraw-Hill, 2010).

6. Unless otherwise noted, the details and quotes from Micky Arison come from an in-person interview conducted with the authors on February 8, 2013.

7. Interbrand's ranking of the most valuable brands in the world placed Starbucks ninety-first in its 2013 ranking. See www.inter brand.com/en/best-global-brands/2013/Best-Global-Brands-2013 -Brand-View.aspx, accessed October 7, 2013.

8. The details of this story are derived from Howard Schultz with Joanne Gordon, *Onward: How Starbucks Fought for Its Life Without Losing Its Soul* (New York: Wiley, 2011).

9. James Dyson, *Against the Odds: An Autobiography* (London: Texere, 1997).

10. Unless otherwise noted, the details and quotes attributed to Tom Steyer come from an in-person interview conducted by the authors on October 4, 2012.

11. For more on Swensen and the origins of his relationship with Steyer, see Sebastian Mallaby, *More Money Than God: Hedge Funds and the Making of a New Elite* (New York: Penguin Press, 2010).

12. Ibid.

13.   Roger Fisher and William Ury, *Getting to Yes* (New York: Penguin Books, 1981).

14.   Unless otherwise noted, all quotes and details pertaining to Stephen Ross come from an in-person interview between the billionaire and the authors on November 13, 2012.

15.   The four-point method laid out in Fisher and Ury, *Getting to Yes,* includes separating people from the problem; focusing on interests, not positions; inventing options for mutual gain; and insisting on using objective criteria.

16.   Michael Bloomberg, *Bloomberg by Bloomberg (*New York: Wiley, 1997), 42.

17.   Ibid., 50.

18.   Ibid., 51.

Chapter 5: Reversing the Risk Equation

1.   For more detail about Yan Cheung, see Evan Osnos, "Wastepaper Queen: She's China's Horatio Alger Hero. Will Her Fortune Survive?" *New Yorker,* March 30, 2009.

2.   Ibid.: 'They had to fight their way in,' Maurice (Big Moe) Colontonio, a paper recycler in South Jersey, told me. . . . 'The Chinese came to us packers, and they said, "Will you sell to us?"' Colontonio told me one afternoon as we sat in the plant office. 'But it was always an old-boy network in this business. I sold to someone I knew, and that person sold to people he knew. And now we've got these people— we don't know them—and they're selling to China? How are we going to be paid? Who are we going to chase?'

3.   http://onlinenevada.org/kirk_kerkorian.

4. Michael Specter, "Branson's Luck," *New Yorker,* May 14, 2007.

5. The original paper was published by *Econometrica.* See Daniel Kahneman and Amos Tversky, "Prospect Theory: An Analysis of Decision Under Risk," *Econometrica* 47, no. 2 (March 1979): 263–91. For a more approachable treatment, see Daniel Kahneman, *Thinking Fast and Slow* (New York: Farrar, Straus and Giroux, 2011), in which Kahneman revisits that work with thirty years of perspective and corroborating experiments.

6. Quote published at www.womenofchina.cn/html/womenofchina /report/123585-1.htm, accessed February 3, 2014.

7. Richard Thaler and Eric Johnson, "Gambling with the House Money and Trying to Break Even: The Effects of Prior Outcomes on Risky Choice," *Management Science* (June 1990): 643–60.

8. Osnos, "Wastepaper Queen."

9. For more on Yan Cheung, see ibid. Will Hutton, "Thanks to Mao, Zhang Yin's a Billionaire," *Observer,* October 14, 2006; David Barboza, "Blazing a Paper Train in China," *New York Times,* January 16, 2007; and an interview conducted by CNN's *Talk Asia* on June 3, 2007, http:// www.cnn.com/2007/WORLD/asiapcf/06/03/talkasia.cheungyan/index. html?_s=PM:WORLD, accessed February 2, 2014.

10. Michael Bloomberg, *Bloomberg by Bloomberg* (New York: Wiley, 1997).

11. Unless otherwise noted, all details and quotes related to Alex Spanos come from an in-person interview with the four Spanos children conducted by the authors on March 25, 2013. See also Alex Spanos, *Sharing the Wealth: My Story* (Washington, D.C.: Regnery Publishing, 2002).

12.   Unless otherwise noted, all details and quotes from Micky Arison come from an in-person interview with the authors conducted on February 8, 2013.

13.   In his biography of Jobs, Isaacson relates an anecdote when Jobs was negotiating a partnership contract between NeXT, the company he founded after being ousted from Apple, and IBM. Once the companies agreed on the deal, IBM drafted a 125-page contract, which Jobs apparently didn't even read. He demanded a simpler contract, and got it, and NeXT and IBM did the deal. See Walter Isaacson, *Steve Jobs*, 232.

14.   Michel Villette and Catherine Vuillermot, *From Predators to Icons: Exposing the Myth of the Business Hero* (Ithaca, NY: Cornell University Press, 2009).

15.   Robert H. Brockhaus Sr., "Risk Taking Propensity of Entrepreneurs," *Academy of Management Journal* 23, no. 3 (September 1980): 509–20.

16.   See, for example, L. E. Palich and D. R. Bagby, "Using Cognitive Theory to Explain Entrepreneurial Risk Taking: Challenging the Conventional Wisdom," *Journal of Business Venturing* 10 (1995): 435–38; T. K. Das and B. Teng, "Time and Entrepreneurial Risk Behavior," *Entrepreneurship Theory and Practice* 22, no. 2 (1997): 69–88; and T. K. Das and B. Teng, "Resource and Risk Management in the Strategic Alliance Making Process," *Journal of Management* 24, no. 1 (1998): 21–42.

17.   Unless otherwise noted, all details and quotes from Joe Mansueto come from an in-person interview with the authors conducted on November 20, 2012.

18.   Unless otherwise noted, all details and quotes from Stephen Ross come from a first-person interview conducted by the authors on November 13, 2012.

19. Twenty-five percent is a conservative estimate. Our study was able to capture specific early employment details for our sample when the companies they worked for were relatively large. When those jobs ended with the future billionaire either getting fired or otherwise pushed out, we could easily capture it. Smaller companies and family businesses were less widely documented, and so in those cases we assumed the billionaire had a lovely experience and simply chose to move on.

20. Isaacson, *Steve Jobs.*

21. Mark Cuban, *How to Win at the Sport of Business: If I Can Do It, You Can Do It* (Self-published e-book, 2011).

22. John Paul DeJoria talks in detail about his early professional experiences working for other companies in the hair industry at http://money.cnn.com/2012/04/24/smallbusiness/paul_mitchell_dejoria.fortune/index.htm.

23. Bloomberg, *Bloomberg by Bloomberg.*

24. Unless otherwise noted, all details and quotes about T. Boone Pickens come from an in-person interview conducted by the authors on January 24, 2013.

25. Roger Fisher and William Ury, *Getting to Yes* (New York: Penguin Books, 1981).

26. Cass Sunstein, "Stay Alive: Imagine Yourself Decades from Now," *Bloomberg Businessweek,* October 23, 2012, www.bloomberg.com/news/2012-10-23/stay-alive-imagine-yourself-decades-from-now.html.

27. Unless otherwise noted, all details and quotes from T. Boone Pickens come from an in-person interview with the authors conducted on January 24, 2013.

28. http://blogmaverick.com/.

29. Cuban, *How to Win at the Sport of Business.*

30. Yongwook Paik, "Serial Entrepreneurs and Venture Performance: Evidence from U.S. Venture-Capital-Financed Semiconductor Firms," Ewing Marion Kauffman Foundation, April 2008.

31. T. Boone Pickens, *The First Billion Is the Hardest: Reflections on a Life of Comebacks and America's Energy Future* (New York: Random House, 2008).

32. For details on the exchange rate for Hugonot shares, see "Mesa Petroleum Corporation" by the Texas Historical Association, www .tshaonline.org/handbook/online/articles/dom04, accessed February 6, 2014.

33. Isaacson, *Steve Jobs.*

34. Cuban, *How to Win at the Sport of Business.*

35. See Will Jennings, *Olympic Risks* (London: Palgrave, 2012), and Edward Merrow, "Understanding the Outcomes of Mega-Projects," (Santa Monica, CA: Rand Corporation, 1988).

Chapter 6: The Producer-Performer Duality

1. Unless otherwise noted, all details and quotes pertaining to John Paul DeJoria are drawn from an in-person interview with the authors conducted on March 27, 2013. The detail about John Paul DeJoria's early professional experiences working for other companies in the hair industry came from http://money.cnn.com/2012/04/24/small business/paul_mitchell_dejoria.fortune/index.htm.

2. The number of Producer-Performer pairs may be even higher than our calculations show. By default, we designated billionaires as *not* part

of a Producer-Performer pair if we could not find sufficient information about a colleague or complement that person worked with closely, and who showed clear Performer characteristics. As a result, our data provide a conservative estimate.

3.   Our research suggests that many of the self-made billionaires who make their fortunes in the finance sector are best classified as exceptional Performers with a strong ability to execute in a specific area of finance. Though some work with partners, those partners do not often exhibit materially different traits—in other words, those partners are Performers too. Exceptions to the above come in two forms. The first are billionaires such as T. Boone Pickens and Kirk Kerkorian who run companies in the finance sector but whose core expertise lies not in finance, per se, but in the sector in which they are investing (energy, in the case of Pickens). These Producers then rely on finance Performers for transactional execution. The second exception is financial Producers who have pioneered a way of doing business or have created a product that was new to the market. George Soros's emphasis on foreign exchange, for example, or Tom Steyer's courting of the Yale endowment as an investor falls under this category.

4.   Thomas Lechler, "Social Interaction: A Determinant of Entrepreneurial Team Venture Success," *Small Business Economics* 16, no. 4 (June 2001): 263.

5.   Amanda Fortini, "Pomegranate Princess," *New Yorker,* March 31, 2008, 92–99.

6.   Adam Bryant, "Michael and Marian Ilitch; He's Marketing, She's Finance: A $2 Billion Mom-and-Pop Shop," *New York Times,* December 6, 1992.

7.   Mark Cuban, *How to Win at the Sport of Business: If I Can Do It, You Can Do It* (Self-published e-book, 2011).

8. Ilana Edelstein, *The Patrón Way* (McGraw-Hill, 2013), 7.

9. The statistics on how much food Grow Appalachia is producing and how many families are affected have been published by the venture. For more information, see www.berea.edu/grow-appalachia/history-goals/, accessed February 3, 2014.

10. Unless otherwise noted, all details and quotes from Herbert Simon come from an in-person interview with the authors conducted on March 15, 2013.

Conclusion

1. For a useful summary on Kremer and the history of RCTs in the development space, see Jessica Benko, "The Hyper-Efficient, Highly Scientific Scheme to Help the World's Poor," *Wired,* November 12, 2013. http://www.wired.com/wiredscience/2013/11/jpal-randomized-trials/, accessed February 14, 2014. For more on school-based deworming, see http://www.dewormtheworld.org/.

2. For more information, see http://www.cgdev.org/page/advance-market-commitment.

3. For more on Kremer and DIV, see Maura O'Neill, Michael Kremer, and Cindy Prieto, "At USAID, Linking Innovation and Evidence to Drive Impact," *Stanford Social Innovation Review,* April 25, 2012.

4. Joseph Flaherty, "Ford + TechShop: Getting Employees to Tinker," *Wired,* May 5, 2012.

5. For more on Coke and Green Mountain, see Michael J. de la Merced, "Coca-Cola Buys 10% Stake in Green Mountain," *New York Times,* February 4, 2014; and Annie Gasparro and Mike Estrel, "The Secret to Homemade Coke: Instant Cold, No Canisters," *Wall Street Journal,* February 6, 2014.

6.   Brad Stone, "Inside Google's Secret Lab," *Bloomberg Business-week,* May 22, 2013.

7.   Bill Gates, "The Internet Tidal Wave," *Wired,* http://www.wired .com/thisdayintech/2010/05/0526bill-gates-internet-memo/,accessed February 5, 2014.

8.   For more on the philanthropic work that Bill and Melinda Gates have focused on for the past decade, see www.gatesfoundation.org.

INDEX